DANGEROUS BLESSING

The Emergence of a Postmodern Faith

Carmen C. DiCello

Wipf & Stock Publishers
Eugene, Oregon

Wipf & Stock Publishers
199 West 8th Avenue, Suite 3
Eugene, OR 97401

Dangerous Blessing: The Emergence of a Postmodern Faith
Copyright © 2005 by Carmen C. DiCello
All rights reserved.
ISBN: 1-59752-259-7

To Marilyn, Luke, and Jake

– My taste of heaven in any era –

Contents

Acknowledgments

This present work is a scaled down version of my doctoral project, submitted in April of 2004 to the faculty of Columbia Evangelical Seminary and to my advisor, Rick Walston, Ph.D., in partial fulfillment of the requirements for the degree of Doctor of Theological Studies.

To this end I wish to thank Dr. Walston, who guided me through my doctoral journey. Rick allowed for flexibility in my program and relentlessly challenged me to sharpen my skills. Thanks for your patience and friendship.

Also, I would like to thank Steve Gunderson, Gordon Nelson, and Stephen Shields for their willingness to endorse this manuscript. All of you, in your own ways, have contributed to my own view of postmodernism.

I am very grateful for the hard work of a number of people without whose help and expertise this manuscript would never have seen the light of day. Natalie Giboney of FreelancePermissions.com acquired permissions, Kimberly Medgyesy provided the typesetting, and the good people at Wipf & Stock patiently worked with me throughout the publication process. All of your efforts have been substantial and are greatly appreciated.

In particular, I must not fail to mention some significant supporters. Mary Kay Walsh read most of this work and was very encouraging along the way. Bruno Tassone provided a listening ear and sound advice on numerous occasions. Robert "Bib" Porter, himself on an educational journey, provided needed "get away" time, most often in the form of our Thursday night movie adventures. Mark "Moke" DiCello has for years interacted with me on various issues addressed in this book. Thanks guys.

Above all, I wish to express my heartfelt gratitude to Marilyn, my wonderful wife, and to Luke and Jake, my fantastic kids. Thanks for putting up with my messy office and the piles of books, and for enduring the many hours I spent in front of the computer screen. You guys are an incredible gift from the Lord, and I love you very, very, very much.

*"You've been living in a dream world, Neo.
This is the world as it exists today."*

Morpheus to Neo in *The Matrix*

"Blessed is the man who finds out which way
God is moving and then gets going
in the same direction."
—Anonymous

Chapter 1

Introduction

The red pill or the blue pill. Which will it be? In the hit classic *The Matrix,*[1] Neo (played by Keanu Reeves) is confronted with a difficult choice. Faced with the seemingly improbable idea that the world in which he lives is a clever fabrication, and that reality is entirely different than he had imagined, Neo must decide whether to remain where he is, in a computer-generated illusion, or to encounter the world outside of the matrix. Should he take the blue pill, his life will return to what he had previously considered "normal." The red pill, however, will open up to Neo the possibility of experiencing life as it actually is. Of course Neo chooses the red pill and with it a mode of living that is no longer easily defined or navigated. In fact he is ill-equipped to meet the challenges of living apart from the artificial realm of his previous existence. For the rest of the movie, Neo seeks to understand and find his place in the real world.

Let's face it. A good portion of the church has chosen the "blue pill." That is, it has decided to close its eyes to what is taking place in today's

---

[1] For a discussion of topics touched upon in the *Matrix* films, see Chris Seay and Greg Garrett, *The Gospel Reloaded: Exploring Spirituality and Faith in the Matrix* (Colorado Springs, CO: Pinon Press, 2003) and *The Matrix and Philosophy: Welcome to the Desert of the Real*, ed. William Irwin (Chicago and La Salle, IL: Open Court Publishing Company, 2002).

world, failing to see that some of its beliefs and views, its tendencies and methodology, are too closely tied to an era that is rapidly losing its influence. Unfortunately, many Christians have separated themselves from their culture,[2] showing little concern for societal norms or else taking an adversarial stance toward them.[3] The "blue pill" is the easy way out. But, and this is the point, it does not reflect the way things really are.

This book is written from the perspective that it is time for believers to take the "red pill," that is, to investigate more closely, wisely, and with more balance, the social environment in which they live, and to consider how best to do theology and ministry today. Of course it is important to recognize the dangers that accompany this choice. After all, changes, shifts in thinking, are seldom smooth and easily managed. Still, it is necessary to come to grips with those features of contemporary society that, on the one hand, call for a response to claims that challenge the very fabric of what Christians believe, but, on the other hand, might provide an incentive to more fully comprehend, appreciate, and inculcate "the faith which was once for all handed down to the saints" (Jude 3).

In *The Matrix*, Neo's perception of what "is" is altered. Similarly, many within today's culture have moved away from the matrix of the modern world and have embraced, often unconsciously, a new way of thinking. This paradigm has often been labeled postmodernism.

---

[2]See Stanley J. Grenz and John R. Franke, *Beyond Foundationalism: Shaping Theology in a Postmodern Context* (Louisville, KY: Westminster John Knox Press, 2001), 160.

[3]This is not to deny that there are occasions when an adversarial stance is completely appropriate (1 Corinthians 5:1ff; Ephesians 5:13). It is just that the church has too often earned a reputation for being *overly* critical, uncompassionate, and close-minded.

"Civilization is a movement and not a condition,
a voyage and not a harbor."
—Arnold Toynbee

Chapter 2

Postmodernism: Historical Considerations

In a world that is rapidly changing, Christians face many challenges, not the least of which is whether they can learn from the ebbs and flows of human history. Is there anything truly substantive to be gained from reflection on what is occurring in the life of a society? Does God teach us through the web of human activity, interaction, and culture? Should believers even care about what is taking place around them?

Observing Culture

A good place to look for direction in these matters is to the ministry of Jesus. In one place Jesus told his disciples, "lift up your eyes and look on the fields, that they are white for harvest" (John 4:35). In other words "look outside of yourselves, and seize the opportunities that are all around you." On another occasion he reprimanded those of his generation who were able to predict an approaching storm yet remained unaware of the much more important prophetic signs of the times (Matthew 16:1-4). Apparently, he believed there was something to be gained from an awareness of historical events. Indeed, one could argue that the basic premise of John's Gospel is to convince people that what could be observed in the life of Jesus indicated his special identity and role (John 20:30-31); in this supremely significant case, watching (or reading about) the historical Jesus leads to a recognition of God's purpose in sending his Son. Among other things, these passages indicate that God was doing something that he wanted people to notice. While there is a unique element to much of what Jesus said and did, he certainly expected his contemporaries to open their eyes to what was taking place around them.

Looking outside of the Gospels, Paul likewise sought common ground among his audiences, thus enabling him to effectively communicate with the non-Christians of his day (Acts 17:16ff). This would not have been possible had he not payed attention to his surroundings. Familiarity with his social environment allowed Paul to helpfully engage the people he encountered. Without compromising the biblical message, and with the goal of communicating the gospel, he was able to interact with this culture in meaningly ways.

On a much broader scale, many Christian doctrines were forged as a reply to those whose beliefs were heterodox. When a teaching was challenged, the church responded by more clearly delineating the truth. For instance, against the Judaizers of the first century, who maintained that law-keeping contributed to one's standing before God, the apostle Paul declared that men and women come into a relationship with God "through faith in Christ Jesus" (Galatians 3:26). What was taking place in the real world prompted Paul to more precisely explain his (and God's) soteriology.

Another example occurred during the fourth century, when the church was compelled to reply to Arianism, which denied the essential deity of Jesus; as a result, orthodox Christology was bolstered and better articulated.[4] Years later, at the time of the Reformation, the Reformers battled against the corruptions that had crept into the church. In response, these individuals taught that Scripture is to take precedence over human tradition, and that human beings can access God freely through faith in his Son. In each of these instances, historical-cultural factors played a role.

---

[4] See, for example, G. A. Keith, "Arianism" in *New Dictionary of Theology*, 42-43. Also, see Earle E. Cairns. *Christianity Through The Centuries: A History of the Christian Church* (Grand Rapids, MI: Zondervan Publishing House, 1981), 131-134.

[5] Because the beginning and ending points of an era are not easily identified, there will always be a difference of opinion about precise dates. This is reflected in this work, for instance, in the slightly different dates given for the modern era.

The fact is, the church has often adapted itself (usually, quite unknowingly) to cultural mores. During the modern period, (1500-1960),[5] for instance, God's people embraced many of the elements of the prevailing era. As society emphasized human reason, individualism, and, due to the creation of the printing press, the printed word, so did the church. These examples illustrate that there is clear warrant for taking an interest in what is taking place within one's cultural milieu. Though caution is always necessary, and while naivete is to be avoided, it is also imperative to remain discerningly attentive to what God may be doing in culture.

Familiarity with the movements of history is very significant if for no other reason than that truth is always embedded in human events. "A gospel free of culture is not a human possibility."[6] Sweet, McLaren, and Haselmayer agree:

> When people say, "I don't want to be a modern Christian or a postmodern Christian, I just want to be a biblical Christian," they are expressing a perhaps admirable ideal that is, nevertheless, naive and therefore dangerous. God's people across the storyline of Scripture lived, worshiped, trusted, and obeyed in many cultural settings–from hunter-gatherer tribes to nomadic pastoral patriarchies, to tribal confederations, to monarchies, to refuge subcultures, to provisional cultures as exiles and slaves, and so on. To be biblical means to live in a culture, including modern or postmodern, and seek to be an agent of Jesus Christ there. Of course, to be Christ's agents in a culture will make us in many ways countercultural. But even so, we are still living out an interpretation of the gospel, as Newbigin said, "in some cultural form." Those ministering in postmodern contexts need a heightened sensitivity to the issues of gospel and culture.[7]

An acquaintance with history enables the church (and especially its leaders) to faithfully resist and counter error, communicate the gospel more clearly, and sometimes it may even help to correct or supplement one's view of the truth. To this end, and in God's providence, it is likely that there are

---

[6] Henry H. Knight III, *A Future for Truth: Evangelical Theology in a Postmodern World* (Nashville, TN: Abington Press, 1997), 134.

[7] Leonard Sweet, Brian D. McLaren, and Jerry Haselmayer, *A is for Abductive: The Language of the Emerging Church* (Grand Rapids, MI: Zondervan Publishing Company, 2003), 84.

lessons to be learned from what is taking place within this postmodern period of the human story.

Of course the intention here is not merely to copy what is popular or to mindlessly mirror what is taking place in society. Rather, God is calling his people to consider what he is doing in culture at large. This requires not only that believers engage society but that they begin to envision the future and what the Lord may yet do. Indeed, it is reasonable to hope that the Lord of history may bring about conditions that actually aid people in their quest for meaning.

History as His Story

The belief that there are lessons to be learned from history flows out of the conviction that history truly is his story. Since God is sovereign, daily affairs are somehow tied to his providential activity. "By providence we mean the continuing action of God by which he preserves in existence the creation which he has brought into being, and guides it to his intended purposes for it."[8] In such a world, God may use providence to instruct his people. Frame asks:

> Does providence provide guidance to us? Yes, in the sense that God's providence provides some opportunities and closes others to us. Yes, in that providence, through our spiritual gifts, heredity, environment, education, temperament, and interests, suggests to us how we can best serve God. A wise person takes his environment and his own nature into account in making decisions. Providence provides the "situation" to which the word of Scripture must be applied.[9]

Still, providence is not easily interpreted. Just because all of life is guided by the Lord does not mean that one can easily or in any detail decipher life's often ambiguous messages. Nor are the darker facets of history, the so-called problem of evil, easily unraveled. However, this much *is* clear: the fact of divine providence is an incentive for Christians to carefully glean from the basic flow of what is taking place around them. It may be, therefore, that the ideas that dominate a given time-period, the assumptions of one's culture, are

---

[8] Millard J. Erickson, *Christian Theology* (Grand Rapids, MI: Baker Book House, 1985), 387. See Erickson's discussion, 387-410.

[9] John M. Frame, *The Doctrine of God: A Theology of Lordship* (Phillipsburg, NJ: Presbyterian and Reformed Publishing Company, 2002), 286. See his discussion, 274-288.

worthy of closer scrutiny than they are often given. In other words believers ought not react to society in a merely negative fashion (though there are times when this is unavoidable) but should view culture as a potentially positive influence for growth. Clearly, God has countless resources, both within and outside of the believing community, that He can use to accomplish His purposes. Kenneson's word to churches is wise, advising that they

> remain open to God's refining work that often comes at the hands of the "other," whether those "others" be Christians or non-Christians. Similarly, churches should remain attentive to the plaintiff cries of those reform movements within and without their own communities, because history is replete with examples of how God has used them to call the church back to a more faithful living witness.[10]

God's presence in and through history[11] provides the theological basis and impetus for knowing the times (Matthew 16:3) and recognizing what God is doing in this postmodern world. Christians, living in today's society, must be counted among those who, like the sons of Issachar, "understood the times" (1 Chronicles 12:32).

Postmodernism in the Grand Sweep of History

Any attempt to capture the meaning of postmodernism requires seeing it within the larger context of human history. Before postmodernism began to emerge, other paradigms took center stage, each spawning particular ways of thinking, each leaving an impression on the men and women of its day.

Of course clearly delineating what these time-periods entail (and when they begin and end) is no easy task, and many different schemes have been devised. Robert Webber, for example, divides church history into six paradigms. The biblical era, according to Webber, "was a time for the holistic understanding of all things."[12] Following the biblical era, the ancient period,

---

[10] Philip D. Kenneson, *Beyond Sectarianism: Re-Imagining Church and World* (Harrisburg, PA: Trinity Press International, 1999), 83-84.

[11] For a relevant perspective on divine providence, see the book of Esther. Though God's name does not appear at any point in the book, his guiding hand is everywhere evident in the events therein recorded.

[12] Robert Webber, *Ancient-Future Faith: Rethinking Evangelicalism for a Postmodern World* (Grand Rapids, MI: Baker Book House, 1999), 14.

spanning from about 100-600 A.D., witnessed the church's efforts to share the faith within a platonic context and emphasized the biblical concept of mystery. Next, the medieval period (600-1500), which was dominated by Aristotelian thought, saw the church give expression of itself as an institution. This was followed by the Reformation (1500-1750), a time when individual believers were empowered to read and study Scripture for themselves. The modern period (1750-1980), following the lead of Descartes (1596-1650), who placed much stress on human reason, led Christians to an empirical approach to the faith. Currently, the "new kid on the block" is postmodernism (post 1980), with its own particular features, which will be discussed below.[13]

While Webber's approach is very instructive, it is also helpful, though admittedly less than absolutely precise, to divide the past couple of millennia of church history into three stages. Prior to postmodernism, there was modernism, which was preceded by the pre-modern world.[14] Following this scheme, a brief survey is instructive.

Premodernism

The early days of the church (A.D. 33-600) were characterized by the spread of the Christian message in a generally pagan world. Through the ancient times, the church encountered heresy, resisted and countered anti-Christian philosophies, and forged various doctrines of orthodoxy. Over time, Christianity became increasingly prominent as a religious and political force.

During the medieval period (A.D. 600-1300), the church continued to grow in influence and power. Along the way, it exercised its authority and propagated the notion that God had entrusted his church with the truth (1 Timothy 3:15). Unfortunately, however, many abuses took place, the church sometimes overstepped its authority, and ecclesiastical tradition was often

---

[13] Ibid., 14-15.

[14] It is important to avoid an overly simplistic or reductionistic approach. One must not reduce human history, centuries of often complex issues, people, and beliefs, to simple stereotypes or overly rigid classifications. However, for the purpose of capturing the basic distinctions between time-periods, the categories of premodern, modern, and postmodern are employed here. For a general overview of the major worldview shifts, dividing these into Ancient, Medieval, Modern, and Postmodern, see Dan Kimball, *The Emerging Church: Vintage Christianity for New Generations* (Grand Rapids, MI: Zondervan Publishing House, 2003), 44.

confused with and more highly valued than truth itself. The premodern era (A.D. 33-1300), though generally characterized by a God-centered worldview and a belief in a comprehensive explanation of all things, eventually produced an attitude of dissatisfaction among many of its critics. Indeed, superstition and man-made traditions left the world in darkness. Consequently, society began to change, and the modern period (A.D. 1300-1980) was birthed.

Modernism

Some trace the modern period to the Enlightenment, the so-called Age of Reason (17th-19th centuries). Others believe that the seeds for change were present as early as the Renaissance (14th-16th centuries), during which time society began to experience an intellectual and cultural rebirth.[15]

For those within the church, the invention of the printing press (circa 1450), coupled with the intellectual resurgence that took place during the Reformation (16th Century), led to a doctrinal revolution. Rather than defer to existing structures, Luther and other Reformers sought to return to a purer form of Christianity based on the biblical text. Just as the world was experiencing an intellectual rebirth, so the church sought to ground human thought and experience in a rationalistic study and application of sacred Scripture.

The Reformation provided the impetus for needed change and was used by God to foster concepts (e.g., the individual priesthood of the believer) and truths (e.g., justification by faith alone) that had long since been buried beneath church tradition. The world was becoming increasingly modern, scientific, and rationalistic. And the church, whether it acknowledged it or not, often acquiesced and came to be governed largely by modernist presuppositions.[16] In this writer's view, this was unavoidable and, in some measure, led to certain improvements. Yet, as happens with human nature, even Christian human nature, mistakes and overstatements hindered the church's progress and damaged its reputation. Thus, it was inevitable that some would grow

---

[15] See Stanley J. Grenz, *A Primer on Postmodernism* (Grand Rapids, MI: William B. Eerdmans Publishing Company, 1996), 58.

[16] The church has not always been aware of its own biases, nor its tendency to mirror the culture in which it lives. Christians have often failed to see that their views, for good or ill, typically reflect societal thinking patterns.

suspicious of the church's (and, more broadly, society's) often overly dogmatic claims of Cartesian certainty.[17] This suspicion fed the human propensity for something new, something *post*-modern.

Postmodernism

Although the term postmodern may have appeared as early as the 1930's, the concept seems to have developed gradually. Some trace the beginnings of postmodernism to Nietzsche (1844-1900). One of his disciples, Michel Foucault (1926-1984), developed Nietzsche's ideas, as has Jacques Derrida (1930-), Nietzsche's "most significant postmodern reinterpreter."[18] Through these and other thinkers, a different mind-set began to permeate society. Most important, perhaps, was an increased awareness of the inherent weaknesses of modernism. With the anti-establishment outlook of the 1960's and 1970's, a new way of thinking began to take shape. This new way can be tentatively referred to as postmodernism. In the most basic sense,

> Postmodernity is that which follows modernity. The post suggests something that grows out of the past but is different from it. The past is never left behind completely but is taken up into the present, even if the present diverges from it or rebels against past traditions.[19]

For many, however, postmodernism remains a slippery term, defying simple definitions, which is why interpreters often disagree about its nature

---

[17] Cartesian certainty, arising from an exaggerated use (even misuse?) of Decartes' "I think, therefore I am" philosophy, is basically a way of describing the certitude and dogmatism that arise from an overly confident belief in one's rational abilities. Of course not all believers were so dogmatic, and many examples might be provided of Christians who did not succumb to the worst features of modernity. Still, enough abuses have occurred to warrant this analysis.

[18] Ibid., 138.

[19] Chuck Smith, Jr., *The End of the World . . . As We Know It* (Colorado Springs, CO: Waterbrook Press, 2001), 46-47. See Smith's excellent discussion, 45-87.

[20] As many contend, postmodernism may be not so much a completed and easily comprehended phenomenon as it is a period of transition between what was the modern world and what is yet-to-be. For an attempt, written in novel form, to think through this transitional period, see Brian D. McLaren, *A New Kind of Christian: A Tale of Two Friends on a Spiritual Journey* (San Francisco, CA: Jossey-Bass Books, 2001). Also, see the sequel, Brian D. McLaren, *The Story We Find Ourselves In: Further*

and value. Some see it as a more-or-less harmful influence. Others embrace it as mostly beneficial. Probably, it is safest to take a mediating position between some of the extremes.[20]

Robert Fryling provides a broad yet useful contrast between these three phases of history, depicting them in terms of "the robed priest" (premodern culture), the "scientist clad in white lab coat" (the modernist), and the "rock musician" (representing postmoderns).[21] Likewise, Walter Truett Anderson recounts the joke of the three baseball umpires.

They are sitting around over a beer, and one says, "There's balls and there's strikes, and I call'em the way they are." Another says, "There's balls and there's strikes, and I call'em the way I see'em." The third says, "There's balls and there's strikes, and they ain't *nothin'* until I call'em."[22]

The first umpire represents the premodern individual, who takes as fact the objective reality of the world around him. The second umpire can be likened to the modernist, whose calls rely on his rational abilities. The third umpire pictures the postmodern, who assumes that his perspective is all that truly matters and that individual biases make the quest for a universal perspective, an agreed-upon strike zone, rather unattainable.[23]

Adventures of a New Kind of Christian (San Francisco, CA: Jossey-Bass Books, 2003) and the final volume of the trilogy, *The Last Word and the Word After That: A Tale of Faith, Doubt, and a New Kind of Christianity* (San Francisco, CA: Jossey-Bass Books, 2005).

[21] See Bob Fryling, *Being Faithful in This Generation: The Gospel and Student Culture at the End of the 20th Century* (Downers Grove, IL: InterVarsity Press, 1995).

[22] Walter Truett Anderson, *Reality Isn't What It Used to Be: Theatrical Politics, Ready-to-Wear Religion, Global Myths, Primitive Chic, and Other Wonders of the Postmodern World* (San Francisco, CA: Harper & Row Publishers, 1990), 75.

[23] While extreme versions of postmodernism are relativistic, it would be wrong to place all postmoderns under this rubric. Though some are genuine skeptics, many are merely doubtful about overly dogmatic claims, especially those communicated in a dictatorial fashion. See Brian McLaren, *The Church on the Other Side: Doing Ministry in The Postmodern Matrix* (Grand Rapids, MI: Zondervan Publishing House, 2000), 166-167.

While there are various ways of grouping societal change, these three (premodern, modern, and postmodern) provide a useful perspective. Jimmy Long summarizes:

> The premodern period was characterized by faith in God and knowledge based on authoritative tradition. . . . In the modern paradigm, the emphasis was changed from faith in God to human reasoning. . . . In the postmodern period . . . we are moving away from reason by the autonomous self and moving toward relationship in community.[24]

The Faith Once Delivered and the Movements of History

Scripture routinely declares that God is the Master of history. In some mysterious yet undeniable manner, he "works all things after the counsel of His will" (Ephesians 1:11). As the Psalmist says, "God is in the heavens; He does whatever He pleases" (Psalm 115:3). Within the realm of his dealings with his people, this is sometimes referred to as redemptive or salvation history. God works through time to unfold his salvific plan for the ages.

God's revelatory intention reached its zenith with the coming of Jesus. Many promises and types of the Old Testament pointed to him. In fact Jesus himself disclosed that he was "the fulfillment" of the Old Covenant (John 5:39), and that his disciples would convey the truth about him (John 16:13) to future generations. Historically, this took shape via the writings of these divinely led individuals (2 Timothy 3:16; 1 Peter 1:20-21), resulting in the formation of the New Testament.

With the completion of the New Testament period, the church gradually came to identify its canon, that is, those texts that were accepted by Christians as authoritative and binding.[25] In time the canonical literature reached its final form, the canon or rule of faith was completed, and God's people possessed the whole of his inscripturated will.[26] Jude refers to the church's reception of

---

[24] Jimmy Long, *Generating Hope: A Strategy for Reaching the Postmodern Generation* (Downers Grove, IL: InterVarsity Press, 1997), 61.

[25] See John McRay, "The Canon of the Bible" in *Evangelical Dictionary of Biblical Theology*, ed. Walter A. Elwell (Grand Rapids, MI: Baker Books, 1996), 58.

[26] In practical terms, each individual believer did not own a copy of the Scriptures. However, the church *did* have access to the written Word of God.

the historically situated truth as "the faith which was once for all handed down to the saints" (Jude 3). "The point . . . is that already in the New Testament period itself, we can recognize clearly the importance of an established set of beliefs based on the teaching of the apostles."[27] These beliefs (which both fulfill and compliment those already found in the Old Testament) are accessible to God's people through the historical documents that comprise the canon.[28]

At the same time, the reality of the canon's completion does not mean that the church ever comes to a full understanding (or appreciation) of the Bible's contents. Christians have always needed to grapple with and articulate the truth. As a result, the faith, which was once for all delivered, must be (and has been) embraced by communities, articulated in various statements, encapsulated in creeds, debated among theologians, and worked out in the lives of God's people.

Though it is naive to expect to arrive at a flawless mastery of the truth, many Christians affirm that the basic message of Scripture is discernable. This is why wise interpreters, recognizing both the perspicuity of Scripture and the limits of one's interpretive abilities, hold confidence (the truth is certain) and tentativeness (some things are not so clear) in tension. It is possible, therefore, to believe in the interpretability of Scripture, while also allowing ample room for correction and discovery. The process by which truth is further uncovered and delineated is sometimes referred to as the hermeneutical spiral.[29]

---

[27] Douglas J. Moo, "2 Peter and Jude" in *The NIV Application Commentary* (Grand Rapids, MI: Zondervan Publishing Company, 1996), 235.

[28] Of course some define canon in a much broader sense, making distinctions, for instance, between canon and canonization, and also acknowledging the practical place of various Christian traditions in the outworking and application of biblical authority. See Charles J. Scalise, *From Scripture to Theology: A Canonical Journey into Hermeneutics* (Downers Grove, IL: InterVarsity Press, 1996). For further discussion on the issue of the canon, see David G. Dunbar, "The Biblical Canon" in *Hermeneutics, Authority, and Canon*, eds. D. A. Carson and John D. Woodbridge (Grand Rapids, MI: Zondervan Publishing House, 1986), 299-360 and Arthur G. Patzia, *The Making of the New Testament: Origin, Collection, Text & Canon* (Downers Grove, IL: InterVarsity Press, 1995). Also, see Kent D. Clarke, "Original Text or Canonical Text? Questioning the Shape of the New Testament We Translate" in *Translating the Bible: Problems and Prospects*, eds. Stanley E. Porter and Richard S. Hess (Sheffield, England: Sheffield Academic Press, 1999), 281-322.

[29] Grant R. Osborne, *The Hermeneutical Spiral: A Comprehensive Introduction to Biblical Interpretation* (Downers Grove, IL: InterVarsity Press, 1991).

The truth can be sufficiently known, though never exhaustively. Our task is to spiral closer and closer to that understanding of the truth that awaits full disclosure at the eschaton.

Redemptive history, that is, the gradual unfolding of God's purposes over time, is basically the hermeneutical spiral on a larger scale. Combining redemptive history, directed as it is by the sovereign Lord, with the fact that the church already possesses the faith in the completed canon of Scripture, the church's responsibility begins to emerge.

> Not only does the theological interplay between gospel and culture serve to optimize our ability to address our context; it also ought to enrich our theological construction. For this reason, we must consider the extent to which our cultural context in general and any particular cultural expression in particular ought to lead us to reconsider our understanding of the Christian faith.[30]

The duty of believers is not to create new additions to the faith, i.e., new revelations, but to better comprehend what has already been delivered to the saints. What this means, practically, is that history is a tool, a motivator, a means by which a personal God leads the church into a fuller apprehension of his Word and so a discovery, rediscovery, or amplification of the faith once for all deposited in the Scriptures. Or, to put it another way, history is the providentially ordered landscape within which God unveils more and more of what He has already provided in his Word. This is precisely why we must allow human history, that is, God's history, to coax us back to the Lord and to what he is saying in Scripture.[31] Carson alludes to this by delineating an approach in which the interpreter

---

[30] Grenz and Franke, *Beyond Foundationalism*, 160.

[31] In the desire to delineate the various eras of church history, it is important not to exaggerate the differences. A discovery (or rediscovery) of a certain truth is rarely *completely* foreign to the experiences of God's people from previous generations. Thus, for instance, postmodern thinkers have led the church away from an overly individualized approach and toward a more community oriented perspective. In the best sense, postmodernism has provided a helpful corrective to modernistic abuses. At the same time, however, it must be acknowledged that mature believers of a more modern bent were/are also aware of this theme (1 Corinthians 12:1ff).

recognizes the once-for-all truthfulness and authority of God's self-disclosure in Scripture, but then frankly recognizes that all attempts to interpret that Scripture are culture-laden efforts undertaken by sinners (redeemed or otherwise), and therefore subject to more or less distortion. It is not so arrogant as to think that all biblical and theological reflection has been accurately and exhaustively accomplished by one group of Christians (ours!), and therefore that the only task remaining is to translate and promulgate the results for the sake of others.[32]

In other words, the realities of human frailty and changing cultural environments compel believers to remain open to new insights from and applications of the Scriptures. Stated more positively, the sovereign Lord works through providence to instruct his (discerning) people in the truth.

Seen in this light, human history is not an arbitrary series of events but is God's way of chasing his people back to "the faith." Taken in this manner, postmodernism (like all that came before it and all that will follow) is the current medium through which believers encounter truth and formulate theology. Furthermore, it can and should be the impetus for turning one's gaze to the God of truth himself, who lives among us still. The Maker and Ruler of history continues to unfold his plan for those who, with hearts in tunc with his written Word, are willing to listen for his voice as it reverberates across the corridors of time.

History and Our Thoughts of God

History does not by itself yield theology. Human beings are not free to manipulate the biblical text. Truth is not to be equated with conformity to the latest version of political correctness. History, however, does provide the context within which theologizing takes place. It is "theology's laboratory."[33] Indeed, no theological system can avoid being historically situated. While this does not leave humanity bereft of anything that transcends its life-setting, it does lead to a recognition that interpreters must seek to properly understand the historical contexts of the biblical documents, the various historical

---

[32] D. A. Carson, *The Gagging of God: Christianity Confronts Pluralism* (Grand Rapids, MI: Zondervan Publishing House, 1996), 540.

[33] Erickson, *Christian Theology*, 27.

situations within which theology has been forged,[34] and the historical constraints that govern all interpreters.

In the final analysis, it is imperative for followers of Jesus to be cognizant of the ways in which history impacts both life and the doing of theology. History causes us to think about contemporary settings (and what bearing God's Word has on or within them), produces inquiry (about the relevant issues of the day), and provides opportunities to question reigning interpretations and paradigms. Sometimes, this leads to a firm refusal to abandon traditional ways. Other times, it enables the church to more appropriately apply the truth within its current setting. Occasionally, it may cause believers to reconsider, add to, or alter their current views. History, properly approached, is the "place" where God allows his truth to thrive.

The church should be stirred by the recognition that Jesus is "the same yesterday and today and forever" (Hebrews 13:8). Clearly, he is a Savior whose presence and power are perpetually relevant. Indeed, this is precisely why his followers must listen to the voices of the past, remain open to the discoveries of the present, and look with confidence to the future. With hearts faithfully clinging to both the Word of God (i.e, Scripture) and the living Word (i.e., Jesus himself), believers in every era can expect to experience a healthy measure of the truth that makes us free (John 8:31-32).

---

[34] For a brief discussion of historical theology, see Ibid., 25-27.

"Wherever there is danger, there lurks opportunity; whenever there is opportunity, there lurks danger. The two are inseparable; they go together."
—Earl Nightingale

Chapter 3

Postmodernism: Friend or Foe?

Postmodernism is one of the most talked about topics in the church today. Though difficult to define, it can be understood minimally as that which comes *after* the modern period (1500-1980). Grenz adds that "postmodernism refers to an intellectual mood and an array of cultural expressions that call into question the ideals, principles, and values that lay at the heart of the modern mind-set"[35] This entails a shift away from concepts such as rationalism, certainty, objective theory, and individualism, and toward those like intuitiveness, skepticism, personal experience, and community.[36]

Of course the real question is whether these changes, those posed by postmodern thought, are good or bad for the church. Some evangelicals[37]

---

[35] Grenz, *A Primer on Postmodernism*, 12.

[36] For further reflections on the changes that are taking place during postmodernity, see Smith, *The End of the World . . . as We Know It*, 45-62.

[37] "Evangelical" and "evangelicalism" are difficult to define. As Webber has pointed out, they can be understood in biblical, theological, historical, and cultural ways. See Robert E. Webber, *The Younger Evangelicals: Facing the Challenges of the New World* (Grand Rapids, MI: Baker Books, 2002), 14-15. Carson is surely right in stressing the etymology of the term. Carson, *The Gagging of God*, 448. See his discussion, 444-461. Also helpful is Alister McGrath, *Evangelicalism and the Future of Christianity* (Downers Grove, IL: InterVarsity Press, 1995), especially 53-87. As used here, evangelical refers to those who believe in the inspiration and authority of Scripture, the triune Godhead, the deity and humanity of Jesus, the sufficient and exclusive saving value of his death and resurrection, and justification by faith alone.

believe that postmodernism represents a trend or philosophy that leads inevitably to a compromise of orthodoxy. These traditionalists[38] maintain that postmodernism reflects, at best, a sincere yet worldly attempt to capture society's attention. At worst, it leads to a denial of the very possibility of a metanarrative, a grand story, an overarching explanation of (and authority for) life. Christians who are overly captivated by postmodernity may run the risk of "forfeiting the integrity of the evangelical truth claim, and the Gospel itself."[39]

For other evangelicals, however, postmodernism is like a breath of fresh air. For them, it is exactly what the church needs, an impetus to rethink its priorities and reshape its attitudes. Though cautioning against the potential perils, some of "the younger evangelicals," as Robert Webber describes them, see the church as more obviously "conscious in its action in and to the world of the new cultural situation in which we live, taking into consideration the new realities of the twenty-first century."[40] For these younger evangelicals, this new phase of history represents an opening for recapturing the essence of the faith, and for answering the cries of contemporary non-Christians who, though wandering in spiritual darkness, are more receptive to the transcendent than their modern predecessors.

Postmodernism, then, has both its proponents and its detractors, each seeking to convince the other that it is in the church's best interest to treat this phenomenon in primarily positive or negative ways. This author, however, will argue that a more balanced approach to postmodernism necessitates that certain features be rejected, while others be embraced. Postmodernism, therefore, can be seen as both friend *and* foe.

---

[38] Traditionalists or traditional evangelicals are those who are, more or less, committed to defending the past and thus somewhat resistant to change. This is, of course, a generalization, admitting many degrees of emphasis. Robert E. Webber defines the traditional evangelical as "the last generation of the modern worldview with its emphasis on reason and science." Webber, *The Younger Evangelicals,* 54. Also, see Grenz and Franke, *Beyond Foundationalism,* 7-9.

[39] R. Albert Mohler Jr., "The Integrity of the Evangelical Tradition and the Challenge of the Postmodern Paradigm" in *The Challenge of Postmodernism: An Evangelical Engagement,* Second Edition, ed., David Dockery (Grand Rapids, MI: Baker Book House, 2001), 53.

[40] Webber, *The Younger Evangelicals,* 243.

Types of Postmodernism

Even a brief survey of philosophers, theologians, and other thinkers reveals a great difference of opinion regarding this phenomenon. Though a good deal of this can be traced to the presuppositions of the individual investigator, it is nonetheless true that postmodernism is a term that is difficult to define with precision. This has led certain authors to delineate various types of postmodernism and responses to them. Millard Erickson, for instance, speaks of "the conservative and the more radical varieties or interpretations of postmodernism."[41] These correspond to what, in another place, he labels "hard" and "soft" versions of postmodernism.

Soft postmodernism rejects those extremes of modernism found in hard modernism: the dogmatic naturalism and antisupernaturalism; the reductionistic view of reason. . . . Hard postmodernism, best represented by deconstruction, goes beyond this to reject any sort of objectivity and rationality. It maintains that all theories are simply worked out to justify and empower those who hold them, rather than being based on facts.[42]

Likewise, adds Wood, the postmodern supposition that we cannot approach life apart from our cultural assumptions "can be taken in opposite directions, one destructive and nihilistic, and the other constructive and redemptive."[43] Carson agrees, separating "postmodernists into two groups–a destructive approach, and a constructive approach."[44]

It is not sufficient, in other words, to simply read an individual's reaction to postmodernism; one must also seek to determine what he or she is reacting to. More importantly, a recognition of the different brands of postmodernism enables believers to more effectively avoid the darker versions while affirming the more useful varieties. With these things in mind, it is relevant to explore the different types and applications of postmodernism, seeking to draw out the positive and negative features of each.

---

[41] Millard J. Erickson, *Truth or Consequences: The Promise and Perils of Postmodernism* (Downers Grove, IL: InterVarsity Press, 2001), 185.

[42] Millard J. Erickson, *Postmodernizing the Faith: Evangelical Responses to the Challenge of Postmodernism* (Grand Rapids, MI: Baker Books, 1998), 19.

[43] Ralph C. Wood, *Contending for the Faith: The Church's Engagement with Culture* (Waco, TX: Baylor University Press, 2003), 17.

[44] Carson, *The Gagging of God*, 77-78.

The Dark Side of Postmodernism

For many philosophers, the basic tenet of postmodernism can be expressed, in the words of Jean-Francois Lyotard, as an "incredulity toward metanarratives." Carson says:

> Postmodernism is an outlook that depends not a little on what are perceived to be the fundamental limitations on the power of interpretation: that is, since interpretation can never be more than *my* interpretation or *our* interpretation, no purely objective stance is possible. Granted this conviction about the nature of the interpretive enterprise, philosophical pluralism infers that objective truth in most realms is impossible, and that therefore the only proper stance is that which disallows all claims to objective truth.[45]

What this means is that radical postmoderns have rejected the hope of (and desire for) any all-encompassing, universally applicable truth in favor of "local truths." Local communities construct their own realities or ways of looking at and defining life, and no one set of criteria exists that is applicable to all communities, i.e., to the entire human race. Thus, it is inappropriate to apply the rules of one group, be it religious or secular, to other groups. In its most consistent form, this has led to an excessive type of pluralism.

Furthermore, these postmoderns advocate extreme measures of deconstructionism. Found, for example, in the writings of Jacques Derrida, deconstructionism is difficult to define. However—contrary to the assertions of Derrida himself—it is possible to say that deconstructionism denies that words actually reflect, in any meaningful way, the genuine state of affairs to which they supposedly point.[46]

Because of the vagueness of language, the imperfections of both writers and readers, and the human inability to escape one's presuppositions and biases, it is impossible, say these pundits, to agree upon anything like a universal standard. According to the more extreme postmodern types, deconstructionism renders impossible the discovery of truth (or a God of truth) via any texts.

---

[45] Ibid., 57.
[46] Grenz, *A Primer on Postmodernism*, 148.

Of course this very idea runs contrary to the beliefs of orthodox Christians, who affirm that language *does* refer to something, that the canonical Scriptures disclose truth, and that there is something (and Someone) behind the biblical texts. Indeed, believers have long declared that the biblical documents are intended to point to their author.

While the church has sometimes underestimated the limitations of human rationality, failing to temper its quest for knowledge with humility, this need not lead to the abandonment of a metanarrative. Nor does an awareness of human interpretive imperfections necessitate an outright skepticism concerning the intent of texts, whose basic meaning is still discernable.

It is on this point that postmodern evangelicals might do a better job exploring and then explaining a truly Christian perspective on epistemology[47] and related matters. There seems to be a tendency among some of them to go so far in admitting human ignorance that they, unwittingly perhaps, detract from a realistic appraisal of the authentic human ability to know. For instance, when Sweet and McLaren declare that "We haven't given up on the truth, but we have come to believe that truth is a lot harder to find than our traditional colleagues seem to acknowledge,"[48] one wonders if they are applying the same caution to their own statements. In other words, have they considered that the truths they extract from postmodernism may not be as clear-cut and obvious as they think? While truth may be more illusive than some evangelicals are prepared to admit, it is also a lot easier to come by than one might be led to believe by some radical postmodern spokesmen.

To summarize, Church history cries out for a humbler approach to texts, doctrines, and hermeneutics. In the process, however, it is also important to recognize and uphold what orthodox believers have always maintained, that God has indeed invaded our world and is quite capable of communicating with his imperfect creatures. While hermeneutical suspicion is valid, hermeneutical agnosticism is to be avoided.

---

[47] Feinberg defines epistemology as "The branch of philosophy that is concerned with the theory of knowledge. It is an inquiry into the nature and source of knowledge, the bounds of knowledge, and the justification of claims to knowledge." Paul D. Feinberg, "Epistemology" in *Evangelical Dictionary of Theology*, 359.

[48] Sweet, et al., *A is for Abductive*, 89.

In fact if no text (or spoken word) points to a reality beyond itself, if it is impossible to arrive at anything resembling objective reality, then radical postmoderns themselves are forced to allow their extreme views of deconstructionism to be deconstructed. Playing by their own rules, they must either admit the limitations of that which they proclaim with certainty (religious and philosophical pluralism, deconstructionism, etc.) or else allow for the possibility of objective truth claims. In other words, deconstructionists cannot actually live according to their own philosophy, since to do so would undermine the assumption that readers can actually understand their writings.[49]

A related contention of deconstructionists is that all truth claims are, at their heart, efforts to exert power and gain control. "Michel Foucault argues . . . that all interpretations advanced to others are in part an exercise in power. They control, define, sometimes manipulate."[50] Greer likewise states:

The real agenda, says Foucault, is the maintenance of one's belief system as the solely legitimate system of belief within a larger community. To the degree that a community is successful in this effort, it will maintain power and control over the larger community of which it is a member.[51]

Thus, whenever a person promulgates a belief system, his ultimate intent is to get others to fall under his sway. The name of the game is power and control.

In response to this contention, it would obviously be foolish to deny the human tendency to seek mastery over others and to bolster one's position and reputation. Still, this need not deter those whose quest is to see things the way they really are. Though no creature knows truth perfectly, it *is* possible, by God's enablement (Psalm 25:4-5, 8, 12), to know perfect truth adequately (John 8:31-32; 17:17). Furthermore, the fact remains that the allurement to power, though real and unavoidable, does not actually prohibit the acquisition of knowledge. Finally, it is important to recognize that the temptation to control is found among all human beings, including radical postmodernists. If their

---

[49] Carson, *The Gagging of God*, 103.

[50] Ibid., 101.

[51] Robert C. Greer, *Mapping Postmodernism: A Survey of Christian Options* (Downers Grove, IL: InterVarsity Press, 2003), 16.

declarations are to be taken seriously, then the books they write and the lectures they deliver are likewise efforts to control. The irony is remarkable.

Do words convey meaning? Is it reasonable to envision a God who is able to express his will? Can even flawed creatures adequately apprehend what a supernatural being desires them to know? Is truth available, and can it be adequately understood and proclaimed without succumbing to an agenda of control and an overriding desire to exert power? Believers down through the centuries have answered in the affirmative.

True knowledge of the meaning *of a text* and even *of the thoughts of the author* who wrote it is possible, even if perfect and exhaustive knowledge is not. This is the way things are in the real world–and that in turn suggests that any theory that flies in the face of these realities needs to be examined again (his emphasis).[52]

History is replete with cases of imbalance, overconfidence, power-mongering, and arrogance. In a fallen world, these characteristics cannot be avoided. Indeed, the church is far from innocent of such charges. Nonetheless, even these dark tendencies cannot stifle the God who, in the words of Francis Schaeffer, "is there and is not silent."[53]

According to biblical presuppositions, the living God is the architect of this world, the governor of all things, the Lord who has revealed himself most profoundly in his Son, and who through his Spirit has promised to teach all who are willing to listen. As Jesus said, "He who has ears to hear, let him hear" (Matthew 11:15).

The Beauty of Postmodernism

Many evangelicals have taken a stand against postmodernism, belittling its radical nature and encouraging others to do the same. Make no mistake about it; hard or radical postmodernism *is* an enemy of the truth, and its darker elements must be resisted. However, this does not mean that every postmodern assertion is invalid or that one's relationship to it must be primarily negative.

---

[52] Carson, *The Gagging of God*, 103.
[53] Taken from Francis A. Schaeffer, *He Is There and He Is Not Silent: Does It Make Sense to Believe in God?* (Wheaton, IL: Tyndale House Publishers, 1980).

Too often, traditional evangelicals have overly simplified these matters by painting with too broad a brush, categorizing all postmoderns (within or outside of evangelical circles) as either enemies or at least compromisers of the faith. Douglas Groothuis, for example, subtitles one of his books *Defending the Truth Against the Challenges of Postmodernism.*[54] All by itself, this leaves the impression that postmodernism is an enemy, and that our basic strategy ought to be that of guarding the status quo, protecting the truth, and labeling all postmodern inclinations spiritually unhealthy.

Groothuis' exposure of postmodern shortcomings is very helpful. One gets the impression, however, that his primarily adversarial stance causes him to neglect the potential advantages that result from a more sympathetic approach to postmodern thought.[55] At times, in fact, he seems to embody the very characteristics of which postmodern evangelicals have become suspicious. Many others fall into this same camp, including such notables as David Wells,[56] Carl Henry,[57] R. Albert Mohler,[58] and, to a lesser degree, Millard Erickson.[59]

In contrast to this mostly negative stance, there is much to garner from postmodernism, and those sensitive to contemporary concerns are better off than those who ignore the issues that have been given voice through the emerging church movement.[60] The beneficial features of postmodernism, which will be explored in more detail below, include a humbler approach to the faith, seeing theological claims not only as dogmatic assertions but truths

---

[54] Douglas Groothuis, *Truth Decay: Defending Christianity Against the Challenges of Postmodernism* (Downers Grove, IL: InterVarsity Press, 2000).

[55] So prevalent is this outlook among certain traditional evangelicals that one wonders what principles and motives have led such a large segment of the church to take this posture. In this writer's opinion, to merely choose for or against postmodernism is to minimize the complexity of these issues.

[56] See works cited below.

[57] See, for example, "Postmodernism: The New Spectre?" in *The Challenge of Postmodernism: An Evangelical Engagement,* Second Edition, David Dockery, ed.. (Grand Rapids, MI: Baker Book House, 2001), 34-52.

[58] Ibid., 53-74.

[59] See works cited below.

[60] *Emergence* is a term often used to describe the new and sometimes unconventional realities that are emanating from people and groups that are postmodern in orientation. It basically depicts the unprecedented changes that are taking place in society in general and within segments of the church. For a brief discussion, see Kimball, *The Emerging Church*, 13-17.

to be further pursued,[61] a concomitant appreciation for mystery, a desire to not merely know the truth but to experience it personally, and a way of engaging both truth and life that embraces the biblical concept of community.

Summary

Depending on who uses the term and the context within which it is employed, postmodernism has been depicted as a time of apostasy and a period of spiritual revival. An evenhanded approach, however, avoids both extremes and seeks to do justice to the complexity of the issues. While not moving too far in either direction, postmodernism is best seen as both friend and foe.

---

[61] This attitude is what motivates the publication of the various "views" books. See *Four Views on Salvation in a Pluralistic Word*, ed., Stanley N. Gundry (Grand Rapids, MI: Zondervan Publishing House, 1995, 1996), *Five Views on Apologetics*, ed., Steven B. Cowan (Grand Rapids, MI: Zondervan Publishing House, 2000), and numerous others.

"Only when all contribute their firewood
can they build up a strong fire."
—Chinese Proverb

Chapter 4

The Best of Times, the Worst of Times: Postmodern Perspectives

Among those who have entered the realm of postmodern inquiry, certain individuals have found themselves, intentionally or not, at the center of this discussion. Those included here are but a sampling of theologians and other Christian leaders who have engaged postmodernism and made a substantial impact within the evangelical world. This brief survey is intended to reveal the multifaceted nature of postmodernism, as well as the variegated ways Christians have responded to it.[62]

David F. Wells

Approaching the subject of postmodernism with a healthy respect for orthodoxy's past, David Wells does much of his theology from within a historical rubric. Throughout his writings, he documents changes within the secular and ecclesiastical spheres, demonstrating the major shifts that have taken place within each.

---

[62] The purpose of this survey is not primarily to evaluate which view is best. While my tendencies and tastes will become evident, the key here is to observe and become acquainted with the ways different thinkers envision this postmodern project. Likewise, nothing approaching an exhaustive analysis will be provided; for a fuller understanding, the reader is urged to consult these authors' respective works.

Wells rightly maintains that the church must affirm and preserve, as the sub-title to one of his books illustrates, *The Reality of Truth in a World of Fading Dreams*. Of special concern to Wells is the desire to call the church back to its former purity and to buttress it against the encroaching enemy of secular thought. Concerning postmodernism, he states:

> Our post-modern world, in its own unique way, is enacting what the Bible refers to as "the world." It is an enchanted reality that has the power to extinguish the reality of God when it intrudes on the mind and heart. Unless we understand this, unless we recognize the ways in which the world has insinuated its tentacles into the life of the church, unless we unmask its deceits, the church will continue to wander in the wasteland, weakened and bewildered.[63]

Wells sees in postmodernism a threat to the Christian faith. Thus, he summons the church to repent of its many compromises, return to its roots, reclaim its intellectual and spiritual heritage, and oppose anything that might distract it from its more noble duties.

Those evangelicals who seek to benefit from postmodernism would do well to pay attention to his warnings, showing greater respect for evangelicalism's past. In the excitement that accompanies anything new, it is all too easy to become sloppy, allowing zeal to blind us to falsehood. Therefore, to the degree that Wells' critique is accurate, his cautions are needed within the church.

Wells' treatment, however, is not balanced, for he tends to lump all postmoderns together. What's more, he seems to approach truth in an epistemologically naive manner. As Erickson writes, "It is one thing to have absolute truth; quite another to understand it absolutely. This distinction appears to be missing from Wells' discussion."[64]

Though Wells would, no doubt, deny that he has a complete lock on the truth, he fails to see that postmodernism, whatever else it does, has correctly pointed out the limitations and imperfections of human knowing. Furthermore, though Wells spends much time elaborating on postmodern abuses, his

---

[63] David F. Wells, *God in the Wasteland: The Reality of Truth in a World of Fading Dreams* (Grand Rapids, MI: William B. Eerdmans Publishing Company, 1994), 215.

[64] Erickson, *Postmodernizing the Faith*, 39.

approach seems to lack "any real proposal for a solution of the contemporary church's problem"[65] as it seeks to respond to the challenges of this new era. Finally, judging from Well's own treatment of community, a common postmodern theme, "There are some indications that Wells has not escaped postmodernity as completely as he would have us think."[66]

In summary, though there is imbalance in Wells' treatment, as well as a tendency toward overly critical analysis, he is correct in exhorting believers to keep their eyes on the one true God and to remain alert to anything that might drive them away from their doctrinal or spiritual priorities.

Millard J. Erickson

Erickson has written extensively on postmodernism, addressing it in both academic and popular treatments of the subject. In many ways, he provides a fresh perspective on this phenomenon by not allowing himself to be moved to extremes. In contrast to some traditionalists, Erickson sees the positive elements of postmodernism and seeks to employ these wisely. Likewise, he differs from those whose enthusiasm for postmodernism leads them in a more radical direction, for he also identifies shortcomings within the stream of postmodern thought.

But, according to Stanley Grenz, though Erickson has been at the front of the evangelical engagement of this phenomenon, he has "at best cautiously embraced postmodernism."[67] This caution is seen, for instance, in Erickson's claim about postmodernism that "the negatives considerably outweigh the positives."[68] Indeed, Garrett claims to detect "a shift from Evangelicalism toward Fundamentalism"[69] in Erickson's writings. While this may be too sweeping a statement, his books do display an overly wary posture toward postmodernism and a hesitancy, in this writer's view, to give approval to atypical movements, even though some of these may prove spiritually and theologically advantageous.

---

[65] Ibid., 40.

[66] Ibid.

[67] Stanley J. Grenz, *Renewing the Center: Evangelical Theology in a Post-Theological Era* (Grand Rapids, MI: Baker Book House, 2002), 131

[68] Erickson, *Truth or Consequences*, 227.

[69] James Leo Garrett, Jr., "Review of *The Evangelical Left*," Southwestern Journal of Theology, 42, no. 1 (Fall 1999): 91, quoted in Grenz, *Renewing the Center*, 134.

Erickson provides a solid evangelical engagement of important subjects and is to be commended for his basic recognition that postmodernism contains both positive and negative elements. Though there are times when he is overly defensive of traditional evangelicalism, his writings are worthwhile treatments of this topic.

D. A. Carson

D. A. Carson is one of today's finest evangelical theologians and apologists. Having written prolifically on matters of faith and culture, his sharp and even-handed treatment of various subjects is immensely valuable. Indeed, he is not afraid to go against long-held evangelical traditions when Scripture warrants such a move.[70]

Among many projects, one of his more profound treatments of current issues is found in *The Gagging of God: Christianity Confronts Culture*; here, Carson provides insightful discussion about contemporary philosophical and popular themes, drawing attention to the positive and negative aspects of postmodernism. On the one hand, he affirms that "Christians have a vested interest in acknowledging that the new hermeneutic, deconstruction, and postmodernity say important and true things."[71] On the other hand, he is quick to point out the weaknesses, even claiming that "Postmodernism as a whole is characterized by astonishing hubris, by a focus on the self that is awesomely God-defying."[72] Balancing these positive and negative factors, Carson observes: "Postmodernism gently applied rightly questions the arrogance of modernism; postmodernism ruthlessly applied nurtures a new hubris and deifies agnosticism."[73]

If there are weaknesses to Carson's approach, they would include an overly faultfinding reply to certain Christians of a more postmodern bent (e.g., Stanley

---

[70] For instance Carson resists the typical formulation of divine impassibility (i.e., that God cannot suffer). See D. A. Carson, *The Difficult Doctrine of the Love of God* (Wheaton, IL: Crossway Books, 2000). Likewise, he refuses to allow theological constraints to force him in deciding between divine sovereignty and human responsibility, preferring to live with the tension that flows out of the relevant biblical texts. See D. A. Carson, *Divine Sovereignty and Human Responsibility: Biblical Perspective in Tension* (Grand Rapids, MI: Baker Books, 1981).

[71] Carson, *The Gagging of God,* 102. See also 96-103.

[72] Ibid., 133. See discussion 133-137.

[73] Ibid., 544.

Grenz, see below), and so a reluctance to spend more time identifying and elucidating the benefits of postmodern trends.[74] This translates, at times, into a "three steps forward, two steps back" approach to postmodernism. While quick to denounce error, Carson seems more committed to defending the faith than he does, perhaps, to seeing the potentialities drawn from postmodernism, especially as advocated by some of its more evangelically-minded proponents.[75] These minor criticisms aside, Carson is to be applauded for his valuable contributions to the church, including his well-informed, biblically driven analysis of today's pertinent topics.

Stanley J. Grenz

Grenz has contributed a large body of work pertaining to postmodernism and related issues. Through his writings, he has become something of a theological trailblazer for evangelicals desiring to thoughtfully engage postmodernism. In *A Primer on Postmodernism*, Grenz reviews some of the history leading up to the current era, pointing out key figures and accenting major tendencies that have dominated the past two-thousand years. Grenz spends a considerable amount of time here, and in other places, showing the inadequacies inherent in modernism and then describing a better alternative, one informed by a postmodern outlook. "The postmodern situation requires that we embody the gospel in a manner that is post-individualistic, post-rationalistic, post-dualistic, and post-noeticentric."[76] In saying this, Grenz does not downgrade individualism or rational thought; his opposition, rather, is to

---

[74] Another example of this can be found in D. A. Carson's book, *Becoming Conversant with the Emerging Church: Understanding a Movement and Its Implications* (Grand Rapids, MI: Zondervan, 2005). Carson offers a critique of the emerging church and, especially, of Brian McLaren. As usual, Carson's insights are extremely helpful, in particular his analysis of the weaknesses found in the writings of emerging church leaders. There is no question, in this writer's view, that such critique is necessary. On the other hand, Carson spends much more time speaking negatively about the movement, and sometimes in cynical terms, than he does exploring its useful features. A more positive strategy (while not ignoring the negative) might tend to disarm his critics and so engender a more biblically-driven attitude among those in the emerging church.

[75] Also, see David M. Mills, "The Emergent Church–Another Perspective: A Critical Response to D. A. Carson's Staley Lectures," at http://www.kevers.net/mills_staley_response.pdf. While acknowledging Carson's contributions to the discussion, Mills believes Carson's approach is overly critical and imbalanced.

[76] Grenz, *A Primer on Postmodernism*, 167.

their sometimes overstated relevance. In these and other ways, postmodernism, according to Grenz, offers the church a helpful remedy to modern imbalances.

Along with co-author John Franke, Grenz outlines a plan for rethinking many of the ways evangelicals have approached theology. *Beyond Foundationalism* represents an effort to move evangelicals around the difficulties that arose through the adoption of a classical foundationalist epistemology.

At the heart of the foundationalist agenda is the desire to overcome the uncertainty generated by our human liability to error and the inevitable disagreements that follow. Foundationalists are convinced that the only way to solve this problem is to find some means of grounding the entire edifice of human knowledge on invincible certainty.[77]

Drawing from Wolfhart Pannenberg and Reformed epistemologist philosophers such as Alvin Plantinga and Nicholas Wolterstorf, Grenz seeks to articulate an epistemology that is not built on any agreed-upon foundation, per se, but instead grows out of "the Christian interpretive framework," as Grenz terms it.[78] Grenz develops his points by discussing theology's sources, which he identifies as Scripture, tradition, and culture, and by highlighting theology's focal motifs, the Trinity, the Christian community, and Christian eschatology.[79]

Postmodernism, according to Grenz, can assist the church by pinpointing its often unrecognized modernistic assumptions and then prompting a return

---

[77] Grenz and Franke, *Beyond Foundationalism*, 30.

[78] The subject of human knowing is extremely complicated and much debated. Some still opt for a type of foundationalism, that is, a way of constructing truth claims on undeniable foundations or principles of one sort or another. Most often, however, this foundationalism is a more modest variety, such as that advocated by Bock. See Darrell L. Bock, *Purpose Driven Theology: Getting Our Priorities Right in Evangelical Controversies* (Downers Grove, IL: InterVarsity Press, 2002), 22. On the other hand, others have sought a different way, a non-foundationalist way, of approaching epistemology. See, for instance, W. Jay Wood, *Epistemology: Becoming Intellectually Virtuous* (Downers Grove, IL: InterVarsity Press, 1998), 77-104, John Frame, *The Doctrine of the Knowledge of God*, 128-129, 386-387, and Robert C. Greer, *Mapping Postmodernism*, 236-237. For a critique of classical foundationalism, see Kelly James Clark, *Return To Reason: A Critique of Enlightenment Evidentialism and a Defense of Reason and Belief in God* (Grand Rapids, MI: William B. Eerdmans Publishing Company, 1990), 132-158.

[79] Grenz and Franke, *Beyond Foundationalism*, 24-27.

to its true strengths. This, with God's guidance, can be an incentive for reexamining how best to do theology, be church, and interact with culture.

In these and other ways, Grenz leads evangelicals into relatively uncharted territory, challenging many of their presuppositions, and suggesting a new path for theology and the church. Yet, as Grenz and Franke acknowledge, not all evangelicals have taken to these reforms. This hopeful enterprise has "aroused the suspicions of those who believe that such a posture threatens to compromise fundamental commitments."[80]

Thus, Carson is quite critical of Grenz on a number of points, even going so far as to say that Grenz's approach to Scripture is something less than evangelical.[81] Bock likewise questions some of Grenz's emphases, though not so severely as Carson. Bock writes:

> I have . . . read with interest Stanley Grenz, whose provocative work has been at the center of evangelical proposals for where evangelicals should go. I find his embrace of so much of postmodernism problematic, for it understates the central role of Scripture as propositional revelation affirming truth and reality . . . . It also understates the roots of how we can know and how we can make discerning judgments theologically.[82]

Concerning Grenz's view of Scripture, Bock comments:

> I am not saying that he lacks a high view of Scripture or that his approach overall is not worthy of serious reflection or is unevangelical. I am saying that his lack of discussion on the role of Scripture is underdeveloped in *Renewing the Center*.[83]

Clearly, some evangelicals believe Grenz has gone too far in his formulations, or at least that he has not clearly articulated some of the implications of his views. However, this does not negate the contributions he has made through his innovative ventures into the postmodern realm. Therefore, while duly noting these

---

[80] Ibid., 11.
[81] Carson, *Gagging of God*, 481.
[82] Bock, *Purpose Driven Theology,* 18.
[83] Ibid., 18.

weaknesses, it is still possible, in this writer's judgment, to say that Grenz has been one of the more thought-provoking leaders of the emerging church.

Brian D. McLaren

While some evangelicals are defenders of the status quo, Brian McLaren is one of those individuals who is able to look outside of traditional paradigms and forge a creative way ahead. As society enters this new period, McLaren believes it is time for believers to reconsider how best to do ministry. "The point is, if you have a new world, you need a new church. You have a new world."[84] This new world is the world of postmodernism.

According to McLaren, the church has often adopted methods that are more a result of modern habits than biblical norms. These faulty ways must be identified and exposed, and Christians must follow a different path. For this to occur, however, the church has to get a grasp on what is taking place around and within it. This includes acquiring at least a basic understanding of the major historical changes, a familiarity with the core values of postmodernity,[85] and an awareness of some of the myths associated with it.[86] Then, having grasped its essential characteristics, it is important to actually engage today's ideas and people. "For Christian innovators eager to build a new church, the opportunities presented by postmodernism are down-right exciting."[87] Among a list of "opportunity maximizers," McLaren encourages his readers "to see truth and goodness where they exist in postmodernism."[88] Though acknowledging the potential for postmodern abuses, McLaren asks:

> Is it not possible–in fact desirable, even necessary–to reject the alternative of selling out to postmodernism and at the same time to reject the opposite alternative of railing against it and attempting to remain aloof from it? Is it not possible to enter postmodernism incarnationally, as Jesus entered our world, learning its language, telling parables that make sense in its context, feeling its pain, understanding its dreams, loving its people, thoroughly in it while not being of it?[89]

---

[84] McLaren, *The Church on the Other Side*, 15.

[85] Ibid., 162-166

[86] Ibid., 166-167.

[87] Ibid., 171.

[88] Ibid., 173.

[89] Ibid., 186-187.

Postmodern sentiments have led certain evangelicals to a humbler appraisal of their own capacities and so a heightened sense of appreciation for the wonder and mystery of faith. In a discussion on the relationship between faith and knowledge, McLaren writes:

> Are we humble enough to look up from the little things we are so proud of comprehending and controlling, to face massive realities–humbling mysteries–greater than ourselves, and therefore greater than our ability to squeeze into our little boxes of "certainty" or "knowledge"? Are we willing to step off the narrow ledge of knowledge to soar into the broad spaces of faith?[90]

What McLaren advocates is good, healthy, and biblical. There are times, however, when he, like other evangelicals of a postmodern penchant, is so excited about the possible advantages of postmodernity that he fails to explain some of his assertions. In the quote above, for instance, McLaren neglects to mention that something like true knowledge or certainty must be admitted by those who embrace a Christian worldview. After all, Scripture certainly promotes a confidence in truth (John 8:32; 2 Timothy 3:15; 1 John 3:14; 4:1-3; 5:2-3, 13, 18-20).[91] In fact the very notion that it is proper to acknowledge ignorance and embrace mystery is itself a piece of knowledge. The point, though, is that human knowledge is imperfect and incomplete, due to human biases, shortsightedness, and sin, and because of God's immeasurable greatness. This should push us into admitting, indeed relishing, mystery and the need for faith. While McLaren would undoubtedly agree with these statements, his explanations are not always clear enough to put sincere traditional believers at ease, those who might be prone to miss his main focus due to their uncertainty about some of the things about which he writes.

To use another example, McLaren asserts that Christians must return to the biblical narrative and the story of Scripture, for the Bible is more than a storehouse of facts and propositions.[92] True enough. But this does not mean that propositions play no role in the formulation and outworking of faith.

---

[90] Brian D. McLaren, *Finding Faith: A Self-Discovery Guide For Your Spiritual Quest* (Grand Rapids, MI: Zondervan Publishing House, 1999), 60.

[91] For a succinct biblical defense of truth, knowledge, and certainty, see Carson, *Becoming Conversant with the Emerging Church,* 188-202.

[92] Brian D. McLaren and Tony Campolo, *Adventures in Missing the Point: How the Culture-Controlled Church Neutered the Gospel* (Grand Rapids, MI: Zondervan Publishing House, 2003), 69-82.

Brian is quite right when he tells us that the Bible should not be considered a mere repository of propositional truths. But certainly we must be aware of those sections of the Bible that *do* contain propositional truths, and of the importance of analyzing those doctrines–for they have ultimate significance for the Christian faith.[93]

In all fairness, McLaren does not reject the notion of propositional truth. Indeed, he states: "I am all for objectivity, absolute truth, and propositions."[94] McLaren simply writes about these matters somewhat infrequently. This is most likely due to his own weariness in dealing with the abuses of an evangelicalism that can be so propositionally driven that it neglects the larger biblical narrative,[95] and to his own calling to lead God's people into postmodern terrain.[96] Though there are times when McLaren might clarify some of his ideas, overall he provides a wonderful benefit to the church by laying bare the weak points and fallacies of modernistic Christianity, drawing attention to a panoply of rich yet often-neglected biblical truths, and blazing a positive and exciting future course for evangelicals who desire to serve God and do ministry, as he puts it, "on the other side."

Leonard Sweet

Like few other popular Christian leaders, Leonard Sweet does more than merely describe postmodernism; he embodies it. Throughout his writings, Sweet advances a positive approach to postmodernism, one which takes into account today's fluid culture and yet remains faithful to Christian essentials.

The church, argues Sweet, has too often failed to keep pace with societal changes, which has led to a disconnect between postmoderns and traditional evangelicals. "Old World Churches," he contends, "profoundly misunderstand the world we live in."[97] In contrast, Sweet adds, "The New World Church

---

[93] Tony Campolo as quoted in *Adventures in Missing the Point,* 83. Campolo goes on to say that in McLaren's well-founded efforts to promote a relational faith "he tends . . . to minimize the importance of the objective truths of the Scriptures" 246.

[94] Ibid., 243.

[95] Ibid., 69-82. Also, see *The Church in Emerging Culture*, 198-199.

[96] See, for example, *The Church on the Other Side*, 65-71.

[97] Leonard Sweet, *Postmodern Pilgrims: First Century Passion For the 21st Century World* (Nashville, TN: Broadman & Holman Publishers, 2000), 141.

constitutes a new ecclesiastical ecosystem that has changed not just how the church functions, but also what it means to be the body of Christ."[98]

Sweet delineates the various responses to this "tidal wave" of cultural transformation as "Denial," "Out of Here," and "Hoist the Sails." To deny the profound changes that are taking place around us produces churches "that have lost touch with the texts, texture, and tensions of our times."[99] The "Out of Here" mentality leads to a survivalist mode and to a form of separatism that "makes Jesus into a Savior from the world, not the Savior of the world. Gated churches are designed to keep people in and reality out."[100] Sweet opts for the third approach, "Hoist the Sails," which expresses the desire to "fully inhabit the new amphibious landscape we live in, even to the point of making some waves ourselves."[101]

Charting a way for postmodern pilgrims, a number of creative strategies are employed. One of these is "double ring" ministry, in which "opposite things happen at the same time without being contradictory . . . Where the modern age was predominantly either-or, the postmodern world is and/also."[102]

Among many inventive suggestions, Sweet employs the acronym EPIC to delineate a ministry model that is postmodern sensitive.[103]

---

[98] Ibid. Though this may be something of an overstatement, his point is clear enough; the church has often been out of tune with society, lacking ecclesiastical maturity.

[99] Ibid., 19.

[100] Ibid., 21.

[101] Ibid.

[102] Leonard Sweet, *Soul Tsunami: Sink or Swim in New Millennium Culture* (Grand Rapids, MI: Zondervan Publishing House, 1999), 27. Also, see *Postmodern Pilgrims*, XVI. There is a sense in which Sweet and others cannot maintain a strict both/and approach, for even the desire to be both/and involves a choice. That is, *either* both/and is correct *or* it is not. At this level, the both/and view has serious limitations. However, Sweet is not necessarily abandoning the either/or approach as a logical necessity. What he refers to is the fact that Christians in the modern era were often polarized by their choice of one side or the other of an issue. For instance divine sovereignty and human freedom were characteristically pitted against each other. For a similar treatment, only pertaining to apologetics, see Ronald B. Mayers, *Balanced Apologetics: Using Evidence and Presuppositions in Defense of the Faith* (Grand Rapids, MI: Kregel Publications, 1984), 197-217.

[103] Sweet, *Postmodern Pilgrims*, XXI. The exciting thing about this emphasis is that it not only provides a helpful tool for communicating with today's culture, but it also fosters a more holistic and biblically informed way of being God's people in the world.

Unless churches can transition into more EPIC directions–Experiential, Participatory, Image-Driven, and Connected– they stand the real risk of becoming museum churches, nostalgic testimonies to a culture that is no more.[104]

Although Sweet is positive in his outlook, he is not naive, admitting, for instance, that "Postmodern culture is rife with content deficits and thought disorders. In many ways we lose as much as we gain."[105] In another place, in fact, he cautions that "Christians should not embrace a postmodern worldview."[106] In other words compromise with unchristian beliefs is not a viable optional.

Probably, the greatest hindrance to evaluating Leonard Sweet's writings is that he is so postmodern that it can be difficult to decipher his claims. While the consistent utilization of imaginative expressions (e.g., chaordic, glocal, edutainment) can be helpful, this is sometimes overdone. One wishes that Sweet would tone down his postmodernized jargon for the sake of those who are committed to the same task as he but lack the wherewithal to assimilate all that he says.[107]

Leonard Sweet is a cutting age futurist, whose aim it is to help guide the church into the world of tomorrow. Though some would question the imprecision of his methods, his message cannot be ignored: "While the world is rethinking its entire cultural formation, it is time to find new ways of being the church that are true to our postmodern context. It is time for a Postmodern Reformation."[108]

Synthesis

As one examines the various approaches delineated above, the similarities and differences are striking. Some people, of course, would advocate one or

---

[104] Sweet, *Postmodern Pilgrims,* 30

[105] Sweet, *Soul Tsunami,* 33.

[106] Sweet, *Postmodern Pilgrims*, XVII .

[107] Indeed, this is a legitimate weakness of the emerging church movement. Sometimes, very little effort is made to "win over" traditional evangelicals. So busy are the postmodern types at reaching today's world for Jesus that they can create unnecessary misunderstanding among those traditional brothers and sisters, who are prone (sometimes correctly, often not) to view this whole movement with suspicion.

[108] Leonard Sweet, *Soul Tsunami,* 17.

two of these thinkers over against the rest. Others would declare that this whole project merely illustrates what postmodern philosophers have been saying all along, that we are unable to escape our personal and cultural biases, and that it is impossible to maintain belief in a metanarrative.

Rather than taking a rigid stance, this writer believes in blending the legitimate contributions of each. From this brief examination alone, a number of helpful themes are evident. These include the need for caution, biblical-theological exploration, and cultural relevance, as well as a spiritual receptiveness to what God may be doing today to transform people, reshape ministries, and add to the church's already rich heritage.

Beyond this, it is at least clear that postmodernism represents both an opportunity and a danger (see Chapter 3). The writers mentioned here are representative of the larger debate as to which ought to most occupy the church's thinking. Perhaps, as well, they illustrate that the church can benefit from this discussion, even if the various adherents never come to a consensus. In light of the fact that postmodernism accentuates community, and in view of the Christian Scriptures' call to unity and the utilization of gifts (Philippians 2:1-3; 1 Corinthians 12:4-11), one of the chief lessons here is that different brands of genuine believers must learn to interact. Ideally, some of these discussions ought to take place in informal, face-to-face gatherings. But even when this is not feasible, those engaged in this conversation should go to greater lengths to understand and appreciate the writings of those with whom they do not necessarily agree.[109] When this takes place, God is honored, people benefit, the truly essential elements of the faith are more clearly recognized and highlighted, and the truth is forged within the context of a body of believers whose individual members sharpen one another in love (Proverbs 27:17; Ephesians 4:7-16).

---

[109] For one attempt to do this, see Leonard Sweet, ed. *The Church in Emerging Culture: Five Perspectives* (Grand Rapids, MI: Zondervan Publishing House, 2003).

"There is something inevitable about
an idea whose hour has struck."
—Johann Wolfgang Von Goethe

Chapter 5

Postmodern Positives:
The Beneficial Features of Postmodernism

A great societal transition is underway, a transition from truth to preference, from reason to experience, from the autonomous self to community, from scientific investigation to the pursuit of entertainment, and from human progress to human misery.[110] Basically, this is a shift from a modern to a postmodern worldview.

As already explained, evangelicals have responded to postmodernism in different ways. Some are suspicious of postmodern inclinations, preferring older paradigms.[111] The more virulent forms of postmodernism *do* pose a danger to the church, and there are philosophical and spiritual errors to avoid.[112] Nevertheless, it is important not to overreact to postmodernism, thereby missing potentially useful qualities.

---

[110] See Long, *Generating Hope*, 69.

[111] As stated earlier, no one fits perfectly into simple categories. However, this group might include such notables as David Wells and Carl Henry. See, for example, Wells, *God in the Wasteland* and Henry, "Postmodernism: The New Spectre?" in *The Challenge of Postmodernism.*

[112] These dangers include relativism, radical deconstructionism, and extreme versions of religious pluralism. See Carson, *The Gagging of God,* 19-37.

It is with good reason, therefore, that the church begins to explore the positive features of current thought. Rather than take an overly censorious view, this writer joins others in celebrating what is good about postmodernism. As Middleton and Walsh note:

> We have found that our postmodern situation, though undoubtedly a time of crisis and tragedy, is also heuristic for a faithful reading of Scripture, pointing us to exciting new dimensions of the biblical text of which we were previously unaware.[113]

Likewise, Smith, alert to the hand of God in human events, expresses his conviction that "even when others can envision only darkness on the postmodern horizon, I see God going before us, extending His love and light into the new world."[114]

Preliminary Remarks

As pointed out in Chapter 2, Christians can and should learn the lessons that come to them through the historical process: at various points throughout time, God has revealed aspects of his character and plan, gradually leading his people to a greater acquaintance with the truth.[115] It is not surprising, therefore, to find him doing the same today.

But before highlighting the advantages provided by a postmodern outlook, a couple of preliminary remarks are in order. First, it must be mentioned that the themes listed below are not reserved exclusively for the postmodern era; Christians from previous periods have ventured into similar territory and entertained these topics. Indeed, to take a somewhat parallel situation, there were Christians before the Reformation who were concerned about the issues taken up by Luther, Calvin, and others. Some of what would eventually lead to revolutionary change had been discussed years earlier by the Waldensians, John Wycliffe, and John Huss.[116] These forerunners paved the way, but none of them did anything quite like what took place through the Reformers.

---

[113] Middleton and Walsh, *Truth Is Stranger Than It Used To Be*, 5.

[114] Smith, *The End of the World . . . As We Know It*, 94.

[115] For instance the early church worked its way through such doctrines as the hypostatic union (the union of two natures in the one person, Jesus) and the Trinity. Much later, the Reformation helped solidify the biblical truth of justification by faith. See Louis Berkhof, *The History of Christian Doctrine* (Grand Rapids, MI: Baker Book House, 1975).

[116] Cairns, *Christianity Through The Centuries*, 227, 251-253.

Something like this is taking place today during the transition from modernism to postmodernism. Though moderns have discussed many of the features listed below, postmoderns are seeking to take these ideas to a new level. What postmodern proponents assert, then, is that certain facets of the faith require more attention and further elucidation.

Second, it is important to note that this project has a distinctly biblical focus to it. The desire to learn from postmodernism is not merely an effort to gain sociological, psychological, or cultural expertise (as helpful as these can be). The real aim is to reexamine what God has already revealed in his Word. If God is the author of history, and if it is his intention, in part, to reveal himself through historical occurrences, it is imperative that believers consider these matters in light of Scripture. What postmodernism does, as all time periods should, is woo Jesus' followers back to their sacred texts. Once there, a number of postmodern themes are found to have very biblical parallels and applications. A postmodernized faith is a faith that learns from what God is doing in society (Christian and secular); then, it locates the biblical assessment of current societal propensities.[117] Thus, with one eye to God's Word and the other to his world, it is possible to find new "resources for recasting the way we do ministry in the contemporary culture."[118] To this end, the following concepts warrant the church's attention.

Postmodern Benefits

Postmodernism has helped the church recapture its divinely established design for community.

Long ago, Jesus told his followers: "By this all men will know you are my disciples, if you have love for one another" (John 13:35). Too often, this has been more of a platitude than a living reality. Much of this failure can be

---

[117] This is not an effort to locate truth claims in human experience, per se, for the Scriptures possess a special status that cannot be given to any other source. However, it *is* possible that the God who works in people's lives can *through* them cause believers to consider afresh what he is saying in the Bible. Furthermore, a "reader response" theory is not in view here, for this inappropriately gives the reader as much authority as (if not more than) the biblical writers. See Osborne, *The Hermeneutical Spiral*, 366-396.

[118] Brad J. Kallenberg, *Live to Tell: Evangelism in a Postmodern World* (Grand Rapids, MI: Baker Book House, 2002), 13.

attributed to human weakness and selfishness. The problem is compounded, however, when a believer's lack of connectedness with others results from being overly captivated by the prevailing unbiblical attitudes of the day.

During the modern era, a great amount of attention was given to the individual. It was thought that the autonomous self was able to accomplish whatever it set out to do. "Rugged individualism" was a popular way to portray the path to success, and one of the greatest compliments one could receive was that of being a "self made man" (or woman). Even Christians followed this route when some within the church began to misuse the doctrine of "the individual priesthood of the believer."[119]

Of course stressing the rights, responsibilities, and needs of the individual is not a bad thing. As a matter of fact, the church is called to respect the value of each person, even as it encourages everyone to follow the Savior. Plainly stated, individuals matter (Colossians 3:12-13; 4:6).

At the same time, an over emphasis on the individual can prove detrimental. For instance when men and women are led to believe they must stand alone, when a *do it yourself* attitude prevails, when people live their lives in pursuit of self-interests, individualism has gone too far. Evangelicals have sometimes encouraged this independent attitude, measuring spirituality by, say, the amount of time and effort one puts into personal prayer and Bible reading. Author Donald Miller recounts his experience:

> If other people were a part of the Christian journey, they had small roles . . . I hadn't seen a single book (outside of the majority of books in the New Testament) that addressed a group of people or a community with advice about faith. When I walked into the Christian section of a bookstore, the message was clear: Faith is something you do alone.[120]

---

[119] It is proper to speak of the priesthood of all believers, that is, to emphasize the responsibilities and privileges of each Christian. But some, in reacting against Roman Catholic abuses, have unwittingly spawned an overly individualized faith and a suspicion, among non-Catholics, concerning anything that is not oriented to the individual. In contrast Luther himself seems to have understood that the "Universal priesthood never meant 'privitism' or religious individualism." See Ed Hayes, *The Church: The Body of Christ in the World Today* (Nashville, TN: Word Publishers, 1999), 61.

It is good that postmodernism encourages the church to return to its corporate roots. As Long states: "The change from an emphasis on self to an emphasis on community, or tribal group, is the primary characteristic of emerging postmodern generations, including Generation X."[121] This means that while postmoderns still want to be treated as individuals, they especially yearn for community.

This community concept is a result of humanity's original purpose. As God's image bearers (Genesis 1:26-27), human beings were created for interaction. Men and women are built for community. Grenz comments:

> As the doctrine of the Trinity asserts, throughout all eternity, God is "community," namely, the fellowship of Father, Son, and Holy Spirit who comprise the triune God. The creation of human-kind in the divine image, therefore, can mean nothing less than that humans express the relational dynamic of the God whose representatives we are called to be. Consequently, each person can be related to the image of God only within the context of life in community with others.[122]

While the image of God is not absent from individuals, Grenz is surely correct in highlighting the social dimension of human nature.[123] Likewise, it is biblical to say that God's design for people is that their lives be interwoven in a common purpose (Philippians 2:1ff), their existence enriched through the selfless use of each person's gifts (1 Corinthians 12:4-26), and their hearts governed by love (1 Corinthians 13). As Paul says, believers are summoned to "preserve the unity of the Spirit in the bond of peace" (Ephesians 4:3).

Without question, many Christians of a modern predisposition were well aware of the biblical injunctions to fellowship, and they sought ways to

---

[120] Donald Miller, *Blue Like Jazz: Nonreligious Thoughts on Christian Spirituality* (Nashville, TN: Thomas Nelson Publishers, 2003), 175.

[121] Long, *Generating Hope*, 136.

[122] Stanley J. Grenz, *Theology for the Community of God* (Nashville, TN: Broadman & Holman Publishers, 1994), 232.

[123] In another place Grenz identifies the image of God in terms of a special standing, a future goal, and a glorious fellowship in community. See Stanley J. Grenz, *Created For Community: Connecting Christian Belief with Christian Living*, Second Edition (Grand Rapids, MI: Baker Books, 1998), 74-80.

implement them. Still, society's individualism often rubbed off on the church. It would be prudent, therefore, for believers of every variety to remain open-minded about the postmodern accentuation of community, treating it as a providential reminder of what God intended for his followers from the beginning.

Though it cannot be pursued at great length here, a number of applications are worth noting. First, believers must learn to recognize their part in a larger body, a group of interdependent people that spans the centuries. Second, it is imperative for the church to make a more concerted effort to embody what community is all about, in other words, to give practical expression to love. This should manifest itself in both a greater commitment to unity and a realization that the church is to be the place where the "weary and heavy-laden" (Matthew 11:28) are accepted and nurtured. Third, believers would do well to forge their beliefs within the framework of community, that is, with greater reliance upon and interaction with other segments of the Christian church. This entails a respect for the church's past declarations and opinions, an awareness of other theological traditions, and a type of theologizing that takes place in an atmosphere of Spirit-induced, Christ-centered unity. Fourth, community must be seen as integral to Christian spirituality. Too often, the church has stymied spirituality through an overly individualized version of the faith. In contrast the church is to be a living organism, a place where connections lead to better relationships with God and others.[124] Fifth, this community pattern ought to help promote a healthy regard for non-religious groups and organizations. At some level, therefore, even secular communities can be valuable, deserving the respect and support of Christians.[125]

Postmoderns desire to connect. They want to "plug into" something bigger than they are, developing friendships, places of belonging, safe dwellings they can call home. In a society that craves authentic relationships, postmodernism provides an opportunity for the church to consider more seriously its community orientation, both for its own sake and for the sake of a fragmented world.

---

[124] For some relevant conversation on the meaning of community, see M. Scott Peck, *The Different Drum: Community Making and Peace* (New York, NY: Simon & Schuster Publishers, 1987), 59-76.

[125] Many groups and organizations have a positive impact in the lives of individuals and society in general. Furthermore, even those gatherings that are normally considered unhealthy reflect, at the most basic level, the innate desire of all humans to connect with others. Christians merely trace this back to its source, the Creator.

Postmodernism has pointed out the need for a humbler approach to knowledge and has resulted, as well, in a renewed acceptance of and appreciation for mystery.

"The secret things belong to the Lord our God, but the things revealed belong to us and to our sons, that we may observe all the words of this law" (Deuteronomy 29:29). These ancient words capture what believers must grapple with in the effort to understand the transcendent-immanent God. Some things are fairly clear and can be sufficiently grasped. Other things are not so clear and demand a large measure of humility, even awe. It is unfortunate that the modern church has often been more captivated by the second half of this passage, i.e., the things revealed, than it has with the first, i.e., the secret things.

A part of this tendency is tied to the fact that the church normally reflects the culture in which it lives. During the modern age, some were enchanted by the pursuit of knowledge, even comprehensive knowledge. Thus, Newbigin writes:

> The thinkers of the Enlightenment spoke of their age as the age of reason, and by reason they meant essentially those analytical and mathematical powers by which human beings could attain (at least in principle) to a complete understanding of, and thus a full mastery of nature–of reality in all its forms.[126]

The church, being a product of its time, sometimes mirrored this attitude, which spawned an effort to construct inflexible doctrinal views. It is not, of course, that Christian orthodoxy is less than clear. The problem is that just as secular thinkers were governed by a belief that science and human reason could solve most any riddle, so Christians sometimes followed suit. A rationalistic faith reigned throughout the modern era. Whether it concerned theology, epistemology, or even the style of church ministry, the rational elements of faith were prominent.

But as history reveals, knowledge is not so easily attained or categorized. In this sense postmodernism has challenged the hubris of modern Christianity, with its neat and tidy systems of doctrine. McLaren comments: "The know-

---

[126] Newbigin, *Foolishness to the Greeks*, 25.

it-all arrogance of the modern world feels chastened in the postmodern world. People are prone to walk more humbly."[127] This, in turn, has fostered a return to a more biblically driven view of learning.

The long history of doctrinal disputes reveals that the grand truths of Christianity, while sufficiently discernable, are beyond total human grasp. In other words it is possible to know *that* something is true, while also admitting that it entails deep mystery. Commenting on the doctrine of the Trinity, Donald Miller writes:

When I think about the complexity of the Trinity, the three-in-one God, my mind cannot understand, but my heart feels wonder in abundant satisfaction. It is as though my heart, in the midst of its euphoria, is saying to my mind, *There are things you cannot understand, and you must learn to live with this. Not only must you learn to live with this, you must learn to enjoy this* (emphasis in original).[128]

While traditional evangelicals have always admitted to the notion of mystery, one must make a distinction between the simple acknowledgment of theological enigmas and the inclination to celebrate them. A thirty second concession that, say, the doctrine of divine sovereignty in salvation is beyond human grasp loses much of its punch when followed by an hour long sermon that portrays this teaching in essentially "black and white" terms.

The Bible endorses the idea that human beings can have a substantial understanding of that which matters most (Micah 6:8; Matthew 6:33). Truth is discernable and God's Word interpretable (1 Timothy 4:13, 16; 5:17; 2 Timothy 2:2, 15). But Scripture also testifies to the fact that all human knowledge claims are partial and limited, in particular those that concern the living God. As Isaiah writes:

My thoughts are not your thoughts, neither are your ways My ways, declares the Lord. For as the heavens are higher than the earth, so are My ways higher than your ways and My thoughts than your thoughts (Isaiah 55:8-9).

---

[127] McLaren, *The Church on the Other Side*, 173.
[128] Miller, *Blue Like Jazz*, 205.

If this is the case, if God is far greater than anyone can anticipate or even imagine, the only proper response is worship.

A corollary to this less pretentious approach to faith is that it encourages greater patience toward others, both within and outside of the church. Obviously, this is not to deny that traditional Christians practiced love. Sometimes, though, moderns have taken an overly defensive posture on non-essential issues such as tongues, the role of women in ministry, and the timing of the rapture, to name a few. It is on this score that postmodern thought has motivated increasing numbers to cross ecclesiastical barriers and begin dialogue. While "tolerance" can sometimes be a politically correct way of excusing ungodliness, a biblically informed charity is part of what it means to "bear one another's burdens" (Galatians 6:2) and show "tolerance for one another in love" (Ephesians 4:2). Humility, then, is an incentive for the believer to first remove the log from his own eye before attempting to extract a speck from his brother's (Matthew 7:3-5).

Of course an alertness to human ignorance need not deter believers from diligent study, nor from the assurance that the truth is adequately revealed to those who prayerfully pursue it. What postmodernism helps with is in reminding the Church that the Lord who is truly knowable is never entirely known. Indeed, what matters is not merely one's mastery of the truth but also the degree to which one is mastered by it. To this end, intellectual and spiritual humility is the ground in which the fear of the Lord grows and so represents the true path to knowledge and wisdom (Proverbs 1:7; 9:10).

Postmoderns long to experience the truth and not merely talk about it.

In the modern world, the emphasis fell on concepts, propositions, and ideas. What mattered to moderns was the well-ordered display of facts. Among evangelicals this resulted in a strong incentive not only to study the Bible but to organize its various contents into systems of thought, ways of understanding what God had said about himself and the world.

Postmoderns, however, are not satisfied with this merely factual approach.[129] As a whole, they are less consumed with theoretical knowledge than moderns, wanting to connect with God himself and to experience him firsthand.[130]

None of this is intended to minimize the importance of truth or of reason as a tool in deciphering it. Doctrinal precision is still a priority among those determined to remain faithful to the Bible's instruction (1 Timothy 4:6, 13, 16). However, the postmodern craves an experiential encounter with God's Word, which is a much more robust and biblical way to proceed (1 Timothy 1:5, 10; 6:3). As Smith writes: "Postmodern people are not moved by reason alone; they also want to know how an event or object is experienced."[131] What postmoderns reject, therefore, is not reason but *reason in isolation*, favoring a personal, experiential faith.

As postmoderns look for experiences, it will be easy to criticize some of their feeble and sometimes ill-advised attempts at spirituality. While a measure of critique is unavoidable (2 Timothy 4:2-5), it would be a shame to miss the opportunity to make use of this genuine yearning among postmoderns for spiritual encounters. The truth is more than the accumulation of facts. It entails a looking *through these facts* to the God who has not only provided knowledge of himself but also transcends any system of thought (Ephesians 3:19). Morgenthaler strikes a nice balance:

Jesus says: "You will know the truth, and the truth will set you free," not "You will have a spiritual experience and your experience will set you free." Yet Jesus did not set us free so that we could just *talk about* a relationship with God. Jesus sets us free so that we could *have* a relationship with God.[132]

The truth is designed to be a pathway leading to *the Truth*, that is, to an encounter with God's Son. Jesus himself said it this way: "You search the Scriptures because you think that in them you have eternal life; it is these that bear witness of Me" (John 5:39).

---

[129] McLaren, *The Church on the Other Side*, 194.

[130] Certainly, many moderns wanted to know God as much as anyone else. The problem they had (have) is that the practices and habits that dominated during the modern era (exegetical expertise, detailed doctrinal precision, theological debates, etc.) sometimes got in the way of this personal quest for knowledge. One obvious exception to this trend is found among more experiential oriented believers such as Pentecostals or Charismatics.

[131] Smith, *The End of the World . . . As We Know It*, 48.

[132] Sally Morgenthaler, *Worship Evangelism: Inviting Unbelievers into the Presence of God* (Grand Rapids, MI: Zondervan Publishing House, 1999), 69.

McLaren is right to speak of "The tragedy of Enlightenment-modernity." He goes on to say that "the era produced a shower of facts, but excluded the looms of imagination and faith needed to weave those facts into wisdom."[133] This imagination and faith should produce fresher and more biblically nuanced strategies for reaching postmoderns with the gospel. What's more, it will motivate individuals and churches to more consistently embody a gospel that fosters and yields experiences with God (Psalms 42:1-2; 63:1; 84:1-2; 143:6). After all, it is only when truth and life meet, when theory is married to experience, when Word is intertwined with Spirit, that true spirituality flourishes.

Postmodernism has generated an increased interest in narrative or story.

Traditional evangelicals have stressed the importance of propositional truth. As mentioned above, facts, concepts, and ideas are what matter most to moderns. McLaren, describing this propensity within the church, says: "During modernity we prospered in the Bible information business."[134] Therefore, the best thing the church can offer is a systematic understanding or organization of the facts of Scripture. In this way of thinking, the Bible is like a quarry to be mined.

Of course it *is* necessary for evangelicals to state the propositional tenets of their faith. Take Christology, as just one example. Jesus is declared to be God incarnate, the Savior of mankind, and Lord of all. On the other hand, these truths, valid as they are, are not the essence of the faith; rather, *Jesus is*. Again, as Jesus announced, "the Scriptures . . . bear witness *of Me*" (John 5:39, emphasis added). That is, they point to him and not merely to theories about him. Narrative encourages readers to become acquainted not only with a system of thought but with a person.

It is thus with good reason that so much of the Bible is written in this way. From the creation and the history of the nation of Israel to the life of Jesus and the activity of the early church, narratives play a major role. Indeed, it can even be said that the early claims about Jesus, i.e., propositions concerning his person and redemptive activity, grew out of the church's

---

[133] McLaren, *The Church on the Other Side*, 195.
[134] Ibid., 195.

inspired reflection on the historical situations in which Jesus lived.[135] Eldredge, speaking of the right way to approach the Bible, writes:

> it's overwhelmingly a book of stories–tales of men and women who walked with God. Approach the Scriptures not so much as a manual of Christian principles but as the testimony of God's friends on what it means to walk with him through a thousand different episodes.[136]

The point is that propositions *about* God require demonstrations *by* God.[137] Descriptions of Jesus' love (1 John 4:10) necessitate depictions of his love enacted (John 19:17-30). Injunctions to follow the Lord call for real-life patterns of what this following looks like in the real world.

This narrative emphasis, without neglecting the propositional aspects of the faith, must be given a place of prominence. Knight makes this point as well saying, "Biblical narratives provide descriptive access to the identity of God. Through the story of God's intervention with Israel and the church over time, we come to know the character and purposes of God."[138]

While propositions grow out of and help to pull together the main thrust of the biblical stories, narrative provides the basis for propositional declarations, containing the record of actual, historical encounters of human beings with God. In other words narrative is not a less significant piece of the

---

[135] For further discussion, see Herman N. Ridderbos, *Redemptive History and The New Testament Scriptures,* trans. H. De Jongste, rev. Richard B. Gaffin Jr. (Phillipsburg, NJ: Presbyterian & Reformed Publishing Company, 1988), 12-47.

[136] John Eldredge, *Waking the Dead: The Glory of a Heart Fully Alive* (Nashville, TN: Thomas Nelson Publishers, 2003), 108.

[137] Some theologians make a distinction between propositions and propositionalism. See Knight's discussion, *A Future for Truth*, 86-97. Propositions are indeed necessary components of a theology that wishes to be faithful to Scripture. Propositions within Scripture (e.g., "Jesus is Lord"), and those derived from Scripture (e.g., "Jesus is fully human and fully divine") are pointers to God, reflecting, in the first case, the actual language of Scripture and, in the second case, inferences drawn from the biblical writers. However, Scripture does not consist exclusively, or even primarily, of propositions, that is, statements about God and the world, but it also includes other equally relevant parts. Genre such as poetry, parables, and the recounting of the story of God's people are not to be depreciated or treated as somehow less significant.

[138] Ibid., 102.

biblical account, a mere means by which to construct propositional data. Rather, it provides an entry point into a relationship with God by providing the historical contexts within which God has acted. These stories do more than describe God (though they do that); they allow the listener (or reader) to observe God as he takes center stage in the divine-human story.

Postmoderns, with their love for stories, have motivated a return not only to the use of narrative as a mode of expression but to the grand story of God in Scripture. "The church's affirmation is that the story it tells, embodies, and enacts is the true story and that others are to be evaluated by reference to it."[139] Contemporary men and women are invited to enter this flow of divine activity, gathering together to revisit the biblical narrative, while also telling their own stories of what God is doing today. Newbigin describes this:

> The person who allows the biblical story to be the all-surrounding ambience of daily life and who continually seeks to place all experiences in this context finds that daily life is a continuous conversation with the one whose character is revealed in the biblical story taken as a whole.[140]

Though the propositions of Scripture must not be neglected, it is also imperative for evangelicals not to ignore biblical narrative. As postmoderns have emphasized, "Storytelling is powerful because it has the ability to touch human beings at the most personal level. While facts are viewed from the lense of the microscope, stories are viewed from the lens of the soul."[141]

---

[139] Lesslie Newbigin, *Proper Confidence: Faith, Doubt, and Certainty in Christian Discipleship* (Grand Rapids, MI: William B. Eerdmans Publishing Company, 1995), 76

[140] Ibid., 88.

[141] Miller, *Experiential Storytelling*, 33. Of course stories also contain facts, facts about the characters in the story, about the theme of the story, etc. The contrast being made here is between statements like "God is love" and stories which provide concrete demonstrations of this love. Both are necessary ingredients in the life of the church. Due to the postmodern celebration of story, some believers are beginning to reinvestigate the narrative portions of the Bible and so join in the celebration.

Postmodernism has helped reorient people to the notion of journey.

Sample # 1: The Journey of Conversion

Evangelicals have often portrayed Christian conversion as a happening or an event. When God works in a person's heart, that person responds and is altered forever. One good reason for this approach, of course, is that the Bible *does* provide examples of such occurrences. Moses was changed by the burning bush episode (Exodus 3:2ff). Jesus' miracles elicited some rather dramatic responses (Matthew 9:1-8). And Saul of Tarsus met the resurrected Jesus and was transformed (Acts 9:3ff). Events can shape the lives of people.

In keeping with this paradigm, modern Christians approached evangelism in terms of a crisis or decision. Those who "came forward" or repeated "the sinner's prayer" were assured of a right standing with God. They were either "in" or "out" when it came to God's kingdom. Jones describes this way of thinking as "Right Here, Right Now."[142]

The problem with this view, however, is that it is too one-dimensional, failing to take into account other ways that people experience conversion. While some come to God through a crisis experience, others, especially those with postmodern leanings, are more receptive to a gradual process of coming to faith. Jesus' disciples, for instance, apparently came to saving faith not via an initial call to believe but through the gradual impact they felt as they spent time with their Master.

Previous generations have, in their own way, promoted the growth of those already converted. But conversion itself was usually portrayed as something that took place at a specific time.[143] As stated earlier, and as seen in certain biblical passages (Acts 2:14-41), many are converted in this manner. What postmoderns emphasize, however, is that many come to God gradually and are thus unable to point to a particular time when they crossed over,

---

[142] For a discussion on evangelism, especially as pertaining to youth, see Tony Jones, *Postmodern Youth Ministry: Exploring Cultural Shift, Cultivating Authentic Community, Creating Holistic Connections* (Grand Rapids, MI: Zondervan, 2001), 110 -143.

[143] Of course some moderns came to faith gradually and not in a dramatic fashion. The point, though, is that the church usually offered sudden conversion as its primary model. In this writer's opinion, this sometimes resulted in a lack of correspondence between the church's expectations and the actual experiences of converted people.

spiritually speaking, from death to life. McLaren, aware of these issues, writes: "I have let go of my focus on 'punctiliar salvation,' a preoccupation with an event or point at which a person 'gets in.'"[144]

In other words methods that operate on the premise that people come to faith via an episode must be supplemented with (not necessarily replaced by) a step-by-step procedure,[145] "a process, a journey that takes a person through stages of spiritual development into a deeper walk with God."[146] This means that the work of God on a human soul must not be defined by the language of transformation alone (2 Corinthians 5:17) but also as gradual advance (Philippians 2:12; 2 Peter 3:18). Peace, in discussing the disciples' conversion in Mark's Gospel, says: "The dynamics of their conversion were quite different in comparison to the experience of Paul. The main difference is that what was an event for St. Paul is described in Mark as a process for the twelve."[147] Later, Peace compares and contrasts evangelistic techniques, adding these words:

> Since the majority of evangelistic activities in the United States for the past fifty years (at least) have focused on sudden conversion (and the methods that arise from this viewpoint), the challenge of the church is to develop more holistic ways of outreach that take into account the fact that the majority of people come to faith slowly, not suddenly. Of course, this is not an either/or question. People do still come to faith suddenly. So we need to continue to urge people to decide here and now to follow Jesus (though we have to do this in a less combative way). However, the most pressing need is to develop ways of outreach that assist people who are at various places in their spiritual pilgrimages and not only at one point (the point of decision).[148]

---

[144] Brian D. McLaren, *More Ready Than You Realize: Evangelism as Dance in the Postmodern Matrix* (Grand Rapids, MI: Zondervan, 2002), 106.

[145] Those who see evangelism primarily as the attempt to bring about immediate conversions will not be effective among non-Christians who are more receptive to a faith commitment that comes slowly and by degrees. A one-dimensional approach has led some evangelicals to use inappropriate pressure tactics. The manipulation of emotions at certain "revival" meetings is but one example of such techniques.

[146] Robert E. Webber, *Ancient-Future Evangelism: Making Your Church a Faith-Forming Community* (Grand Rapids, MI: Baker books, 2003), 129.

[147] Richard V. Peace, *Conversion in the New Testament: Paul and the Twelve* (Grand Rapids, MI: William B. Eerdmans Publishing Company, 1999), 106.

[148] Ibid., 286-287.

Sample # 2: The Journey of Theology

Within the realm of theology, something similar has occurred. As Christians sought to frame the truth in doctrinal statements, they were prone to dogmatism. In the pursuit and defense of orthodoxy, various schools of theology treated their versions of the faith as something of a final product. Osborne observes:

> The basic problem of theological models is the tendency of their adherents to give an absolute or permanent status that often becomes more powerful than Scripture itself. This is demonstrated in the tendency of all traditions to interpret Scripture on the basis of their beliefs rather than to examine their systems and alter them on the basis of the scriptural evidence.[149]

Postmoderns, more than those who came before them, are suspicious of overly confident assertions, opting for a more modest approach to truth. Though some have taken this humbler stance to an extreme, succumbing, for instance, to relativism, many do not go nearly this far. McLaren says:

> What postmodern people tend to reject is not absolute truth, but absolute knowledge. And to the degree we seek to defend absolute knowledge, we show ourselves to be defenders not of biblical faith (which repeatedly affirms that we "know in part") but of modern rationalism (which displays an overconfidence about its autonomous powers of knowledge that is hard to overexaggerate).[150]

If this assessment is accurate, truth is not merely a commodity to be easily located and precisely understood. Though "the faith once for all delivered" (Jude 3) is clear enough to be perceived and applied, the church's understanding of it is always imperfect (and sometimes flawed). All too often in the modern world, there was a close-mindedness among evangelicals and an unnecessary disconnect within the body of Christ. Thus, Calvinists opposed Arminans, and vice versa. Dispensationalists debated those who held to Covenant theology. Cessaionionists separated from non-cessasionists. It is not that healthy discussion (and even disagreement) is inappropriate, but that

---

[149] Osborne, *The Hermeneutical Spiral*, 304.
[150] McLaren, *The Church on the Other Side*, 166.

it often degenerated into an arrogant separatist attitude. With regard to theological systems, Osborne wisely suggests that "we must allow the text to challenge, clarify and if necessary change the very system [of theology]. The continuous interaction between text and system forms a spiral upward to theological truth."[151] Brian McLaren provides these insightful words:

> This, to me, is a wonderful sign of wisdom and growth–to hold beliefs that puzzle you, and to be puzzled by beliefs that hold you. This is the vital sign of a vibrant faith of heart and head, a dynamic faith that isn't brain-dead, hasn't committed intellectual suicide, and is in process.[152]

Indeed, the ongoing effort to unfold the truth is what God desires. As Chris Seay affirms, "Jesus understood that it's not only the truth that changes us, but also the *journey* of seeking it."[153]

In summary, there is much to learn from the postmodern emphasis on process. Evangelistically, rather than approaching people in terms of a decision to believe, it can often be better to simply walk with them, inviting them on a spiritual journey. This allows God to renew individuals at a pace that best fits their needs and in a way that perpetuates a continual spiritual encounter. Likewise, theologically, the formulation of truth is a on-going affair, requiring a respect for historic orthodoxy, a cognizance of other theological schools of thought, and, most importantly, an openness to what God through his Spirit might yet reveal through his Word.

Postmoderns, then, join discerning believers of previous times in contributing to a more fully orbed faith perspective. From the vantage point of postmodernity, comprehension is procured through pilgrimage, transformation occurs over time, and the church is led gradually yet surely, imperfectly yet adequately, toward its completion, when Jesus returns and his followers "see Him just as He is" (1 John 3:2).

---

[151] Osborne, *The Hermeneutical Spiral*, 304.

[152] McLaren, *More Ready Than You Realize*, 115.

[153] Chris Seay, "I Have Inherited the Faith of My Fathers" in *Stories of Emergence: Moving From Absolute To Authentic* (Grand Rapids, MI: Zondervan Publishing House, 2003), 79.

Conclusion

Heraclitus once remarked, "You cannot twice step into the same river, for other waters are continually flowing on."[154] Likewise, societal customs, philosophical assumptions, trends, and even people themselves change.

Of course the contention of orthodox believers is that these historical permutations are orchestrated by a sovereign God. The Lord of the ages governs history. Indeed, his presence can be detected in every time period, including this present one. God, therefore, must be doing something during this postmodern phase of the church.

The thesis put forth here is that there are aspects of postmodernism that should be welcomed by followers of Christ. These have the potential not only of stimulating relevant conversation but also of leading the church into a fuller perception and application of the truth. That is to say, the best kind of postmodernism actually draws to the surface and reinforces basic Christian beliefs.

Among many benefits, postmodernism has fostered a deeper sense of community, a humbler approach to knowledge, an increased desire to experience the faith, and not merely know about it, a greater appropriation of the grand biblical story, and a healthier awareness of the progressive nature of the Christian journey. These and other factors remind believers that God is still at work today. McNeal, in fact, maintains that

> The postmodern world, governed by quantum physics and its emphasis on relationships, is God's end run around the modern world. . . . God himself is stirring the pot. If we can pay attention we will eventually discover that not only will we not lose God in this emerging postmodern world, we will find him again![155]

While it is essential to resist radical postmodernism, a number of beneficial themes have assisted the church in coming to a more holistic view of the faith. Those who pay attention can greatly benefit from these postmodern positives.

---

[154] Heraclitus as quoted in George Sweeting, *Who Said That?* (Chicago, IL: Moody Press, 1995), 79.

[155] Reggie McNeal, *The Present Future: Six Tough Questions for the Church* (San Francisco, CA: Jossey-Bass Books, 2003), 6.

There is a tide in the affairs of men,
Which taken at the flood, leads on to fortune;
Omitted, all the voyage of their life
Is bound in shallows and in miseries.
On such a full sea are we now afloat;
And we must take the current when it serves,
Or lose our ventures.
—William Shakespeare, Brutus, in Julius Caesar

Chapter 6

Postmodernism: Dangerous Blessing

To categorize postmodernism as simply a virtue or a vice is far too simplistic. Truth and error exist side-by-side in this world. Opposing forces are at work, both spiritual and intellectual in nature, both theoretical and practical. Sometimes, in fact, these show up in the same places and among the same writers. In the ongoing quest to learn how best to live and think as Christians in today's world, it is imperative that postmodernism be approached in a simultaneously open and careful way.

Those on both sides of this debate have frequently defended opposite yet equally incomplete views. Some postmodern believers have been guilty of a politically correct attitude toward trends, a tendency to over simplify, a shoddy handling of biblical texts, a lack of respect for the exegetical and theological claims of previous generations, and a general failure to recognize that today's "cutting edgers" will one day be the object of critique and, perhaps, criticism. Here is where postmodern evangelicals must avoid the very hubris for which they have corrected their modern predecessors. Postmodernism may be a time of great movements by God, a time of much needed reformation, but it is not the golden age that awaits the eschaton.

Traditional evangelicals, on the other hand, in particular those who have simply dismissed postmodernism without a fair hearing, are prone to overstate their views, take a reactionary stance to anything new, distance themselves from those whom Jesus loves, and confuse modern assumptions *about* God's Word with what his Word actually says.

As followers of Jesus enter this postmodern stage of history, it will be necessary to employ all of the spiritual, theological, and community resources that are available. In this writer's view, this leads to a positive attitude toward this time in which we live, coupled with a sufficient alertness to the potential hindrances that can be located within culture, the church, and our own hearts.

Poe correctly notes: "Our experience with postmodernism will largely depend on whether we view postmodern people as an enemy or an opportunity."[156] More so, our outlook will depend on whether we regard this era as an evil to be resisted or an opportunity to be exploited. And this is precisely where the tensions lie, for postmodernism can be treated as either a danger or a blessing.

The approach advocated here, however, recognizes that both negative and positive traits permeate every human society. Therefore, Christians would be wise to see postmodernism as a dangerous blessing. While rejecting as antithetical to Christian orthodoxy the more pernicious forms of postmodernism, a properly nuanced postmodernization of evangelicalism is apropos, for "postmodern philosophy might provide a long awaited remedy to a Christianity grown somewhat ill through an overdose of modernity."[157] In this scenario, though remaining cognizant of the theological and moral risks that face the church, it is possible to align ourselves with those who recognize in this time an occasion to unite in love, reflect on faith, and journey together into the postmodern world and beyond.

---

[156] Harry Lee Poe, *Christian Witness in a Postmodern World* (Nashville, TN: Abington Press, 2001), 171.

[157] Kallenberg, *Live to Tell*, 13.

Appendix A

Avoiding Naivete and Worldliness

There has sometimes been a suspicion among traditional evangelicals about those influenced by postmodern thought. Such a step might be construed as a move away from God and toward worldliness. Considering the seriousness of this accusation and the genuine danger of succumbing to worldliness, a biblically-focused excursus is apropos.

"Do not love the world nor the things in the world. If anyone loves the world, the love of the Father is not in him" (1 John 2:15). With these words, John warns his readers that conformity to the world is antithetical to God's purpose for his followers. According to John, no one can simultaneously love God and the world.[158]

Worldliness is a common biblical theme. Indeed, there is a clear distinction in Scripture between people who are governed by "the spirit of the world" and those who are recipients of "the Spirit who is from God" (1 Corinthians 2:12). Thus, God's desire, James writes, is that Christians remain "unstained by the world" (James 1:27). Likewise, he bluntly exclaims: "Do you not know that friendship with the world is hostility toward God? Therefore whoever wishes to be a friend of the world makes himself an enemy of God" (James 4:4). Plainly,

---

[158] See Colin G. Kruse, "The Letters of John" in *The Pillar New Testament Commentary* (Grand Rapids, MI: William B. Eerdmans Publishing Company, 2000), 94-97.

God despises anything that attempts to compete with him for our affection, for this amounts to idolatry. Worldliness is treated in such a negative manner precisely because it is the very opposite of what God's wants for (and from) us.

Of course what it means to be worldly cannot be summarized by simplistic prohibitions. "Don't drink, smoke, swear, or go to movies" hardly captures the heart of the matter,[159] for worldliness is more a matter of wrong priorities than arbitrarily imposed requirements.[160] Indeed, it involves a conformity to anti-God attitudes and behaviors, the absorption of a mind set and way of life that is characteristic of those who think their thoughts and live their lives with no reference to God. If the world moves away from God, it is clear that those who follow the world will do likewise.

All of this impacts the way Christians approach and interact with culture. At the very least, it implies that any thoughtful inspection of society (or, of the church, for that matter) must contain an element of caution (Ephesians 5:15-17). In a world that is governed by dark spiritual forces (Ephesians 6:10ff), and in which human beings are liable to deception (Jeremiah 17:9), it is imperative to remain careful about what is assimilated along the way (Proverbs 4:23). In our desire to interact with postmodern themes, we must not allow the more damaging features of postmodern society to bewitch us. While cultural analysis is both necessary and potentially healthy, it is never an excuse for compromise.

Many scholars and lay people agree that postmodernism emphasizes the need for community and the importance of maintaining a humble posture in all human endeavors.[161] To that end, the church must learn to take this

---

[159] This is not to deny that certain activities are indeed inappropriate for Christians. Nor does it negate the basic principle that a person ought to avoid whatever causes him to stumble or act in ways that are contrary to faith. The point being made here is simply that, whatever the precise choices one makes, holiness is a process that originates in the heart. Likewise, worldliness is first of all an inward disposition.

[160] See Tom Hovestol, *Extreme Righteousness: Seeing Ourselves in the Pharisees* (Chicago, IL: Moody Press, 1997), 139.

[161] At this juncture, a distinction should be made between postmodernism and postmoderns. Postmodernism favors a modest attitude toward life, which is a good thing. Postmoderns, on the other hand, are as prone to arrogance as their predecessors. Thus, while postmodern individuals may espouse a humbler theory of knowledge, they are just as liable to conceit as anyone else. A parallel can be found in discussing Calvinism. Though Calvinism claims adherence to doctrines that lead away from pride, Calvinists are not immune from haughtiness.

postmodern journey together, relying on one another and the Spirit of God, and looking with prayerful hearts to the Savior who came to save us from our sin (Matthew 1:21), including the sin that results from naivete and worldliness.

Appendix B

A Fifth Way?

A (Sort of) Different Approach to Postmodernism

As history takes a postmodern turn, it is not completely clear how best to respond to today's cataclysmic cultural shifts. Evangelicals are far from united in the ways they tackle these changes, with various authors proposing different approaches to postmodern trends.

Of course categorizing the various evangelical views is no simple task, for rarely do any two writers completely agree. What I propose here, therefore, is a very generalized perspective on the responses of evangelicals to postmodernism. Clearly, there is overlap in the categories (and among the various adherents), and I claim no special insight into the hearts of those who seek to engage culture.

With these limitations clearly in place, what follows is a basic grouping of evangelical stances to the changes that are taking place in today's world. Though this analysis is somewhat simplistic, I have detected the following reactions to postmodernism.

1. "Defend and Attack"

Some evangelicals are clearly defenders of the status quo. For whatever legitimate or illegitimate reasons, they are critical of anything that might disturb ministry as they envision it. As such, these Christians are vigilant in their efforts to shield the church from the errors of postmodern thought.

One example of this type of response is found in the writings of David Wells, who sees in postmodernism a threat to the faith. According to Wells, those who get tangled in the web of postmodern philosophy are opening themselves to compromise, or worse apostasy.

While not all evangelicals fit within this rubric, it is a fairly common response among traditional believers. Many Christians see themselves as protectors of the faith and, thus, feel the need to reject anything that, in their opinion, sounds too postmodern.

Benefits: Avoids certain dangers found in culture. Stays away from worldliness as traditionally defined.

Disadvantages: Tends to be overly critical ("Throwing out the baby with the bath water"). Can lead to pride ("We have the answers, and you don't."). Misses potential evangelistic opportunities.

2. "When in Rome"

Another branch of Christendom, however, is not so critical of what it taking place in our society. These individuals feel a strong calling to reach non-Christians with the gospel. As a result, they are prone to see postmodernism as little more than a matter of form. If music styles change, then we must adapt to these changes for the sake of those who don't yet know Jesus. If young people begin to speak a different language, we should learn to speak that language too.

One apparent example of this is found in the so-called seeker sensitive movement. These evangelicals (e.g., Rick Warren?) do what they can to promote an atmosphere that is comfortable for outsiders. Thus, the gospel is presented in a way that is easily accessible to our contemporaries.

This response to postmodernism best fits the "When in Rome" model, for it recognizes that cultural change requires that Christians make appropriate adaptations. When in Rome, or in a postmodern world, you need to do whatever fosters better communication.

Benefits: Makes connection with postmoderns. Picks up on certain positive postmodern tendencies.

Disadvantages: Sometimes underestimates the degree of change (whether good or bad) taking place in society and the implications for theology and life.

3. "Two Steps Forward, Three Steps Back"

The third response in some ways resembles the previous model (# 2). The difference is that this type of reply to postmodernism tends to be a bit more critical of (even cynical toward) the negative postmodern tendencies.

D. A. Carson and Millard Erikson seem to fit this mold. On the one hand, they are concerned–like the "When in Rome Approach" advocates–to reach today's generation with the good news. If we can benefit from postmodern themes and from a proper critique of modernism's bad points, we ought to do so. On the other hand, there is also a proneness among these evangelicals to be wary of anything that might lead us astray. Thus, in this writer's opinion at least, there is this tendency to acknowledge some of the potential benefits of postmodernity ("Two Steps Forward") but to do so with great caution and in such a way that the dangers of postmodernity get more ink than the positive features ("Three Step Back").

Benefits: Notices at least some of the changes that need to me made in order to reach postmoderns. Quick to point out and caution the church about the dangers of postmodernity.

Disadvantages: Promotes an "us-them" mentality within evangelicalism ("We traditionalists are the experts, and you non-traditionalists could learn something from us."). Confuses "university driven" postmodernism (e.g., Jacques Derrida) with "street level" versions of the same (e.g., your neighbor). Sounds arrogant to many (both within and outside of the church). Though admitting postmodern benefits, tends to neglect any prolonged discussion of these benefits.

4. "No Looking Back"

Another response to postmodernism takes a different path. Those who follow the "No Looking Back" motto are simply excited about what God is doing in our culture today. Many within the emerging church fit broadly into this category. Of course for some, postmodernism is simply the next "cool" thing to do. For others, however, it has been the impetus for great change and the motivation for a renewed faith commitment.

Leonard Sweet might be one of the more popular representatives of this group, though others are more radical in their approach than he. The idea is that if God is "out there" in our postmodern world, and if he is challenging our beliefs and practices, so be it. Let's take the postmodern plunge!

Benefits: Cutting edge. Conducive approach for reaching postmoderns with the gospel. Open to what God is doing in society today. Aware of evangelicalism's "captivity" to modern ideals. Conversant with relevant postmodern themes.

Disadvantages: Too quickly dismisses the past (e.g., modernism), failing to see that God has left his mark in previous eras. Theologically and exegetically shallow at times. Sometimes comes across as "politically correct" and condescending ("Oh, those poor traditional evangelicals just don't get it.").

It is quite likely that the previous depictions are less than precise, and it may even be that I have misrepresented an evangelical or two. For this, I apologize. My intent, simply, is to point out some of the ways in which evangelicals have approached postmodernity.

Having said this, I have to admit that I don't quite fit any of the paradigms listed above. While aspects of each of these proposals resonate with me, I'm still searching for another way, a fifth way.

5. A Fifth Way: "The Best of All Worlds"

The fifth way that I am proposing in not so much a settled view as it is on-going (which I realize is a very postmodern idea). In saying this, I accept, in varying degrees, at least some of what is proposed by each of the above views. "Defend and attack" has its place, though not as much a place, in my opinion, as some people tend to think; it also preserves a theological outlook often lacking in other views. "When in Rome" represents an essential aspect of Christian mission, which must always be concerned with reaching others with the gospel. "Two Steps Forward, Three Steps Back" reminds me of the tension that attends all efforts to be faithful in a fallen world; though this view is too limiting for my liking, it does serve to demonstrate that our journey through this world is a dangerous one. Finally, the "No Looking Back" model, though sometimes naive, is a necessary incentive for anyone desiring, as I do, to connect with what God is doing in our midst.

Of all of these views, I suppose the last two (3 and 4) best fit my current way of thinking. In saying this, though, I am still very much frustrated with the tendency, at least as I perceive it, to miss part of the big picture. Thus, for instance, when I read postmodern types, I often detect an ignorance of theology and exegesis, a proneness to choose the worst examples of modern evangelicalism (often, I suspect, because these individuals were "victims" of such faulty ministries), an amazing naivete when it comes to the greater flow of redemptive history (i.e., one day, *we* might be considered the "traditionalists," and surely we are not living in some sort of golden age), a simplistic use of postmodern themes (How many times do I have to **read** about the demise of the printed word? If you're writing about it, it hasn't gone away just yet!), a tendency to give mere lip service to the achievements of previous generations (It is one thing to say that we are not rejecting modernism outright but simply building on it. It is quite another thing to actually make use of, say, reason and logic, "modern" traits that still serve us well in a postmodern world), and an apparent lack of awareness of its own form of pride.

Then again, when I read the better informed traditionalists, I am just as frustrated (if not more so) with their smug attitudes and subtle (or not so subtle) superiority complex. Somehow, traditional evangelicals believe that it's up to them to keep the faithful on track. Likewise, I see a tendency to model (and so incite) anxiety among evangelicals, who are so afraid of neglecting to cross a theological "T" that they fail to open their eyes to what is taking place all around them. If God is, in some manner, at work via the emergent movement, how "Pharisaic" it is for traditional evangelicals to think that they are the guardians of the faith and protectors of the truth. In my opinion, much of evangelicalism is "out of touch," corny, silly-looking, defensive, overly theoretical (at the expense of experience), too individualistic, and just plain arrogant. If this is even partially true, why cannot traditional evangelicals humble themselves enough to admit the possibility that postmodernism (in its best forms) may be at least one way among others of achieving greater faithfulness and more balance?

What I see, therefore, is a tendency to go in one direction or the other, and this, as I've said, is disconcerting. Can we not at least try to locate a better way? Without appearing arrogant (which I may already be), I'm looking for something different, and I long to find fellow companions who feel the same way. I am tired of the traditional response to postmodernism, and I'm not interested in a half-hearted, fearful approach to today's trends. I want to wholeheartedly embrace and embody the best kind of postmodern ministry. At the same time, I am not interested in a postmodernism ministry that is intellectually lazy, nor one that comes across as trendy, condescending (toward moderns), acts like it has already arrived at the eschaton, and doesn't even bother to attract modern types in a more postmodern direction. God save us from postmodern hubris (ironic, isn't it?)!

Can't we, in good postmodern fashion, truly seek to embrace the best of all worlds? Is it not possible to hear the concerns of a D. A. Carson, follow the inclinations of a Brian McLaren, and dare set sail with a Len Sweet? To be honest, I don't know where I am in all this. But I do know that God is governing our lives, including the direction of this and every culture. Therefore, it is clear to me that we need his wisdom if we are going to navigate this strange and wonderful, dangerous and blessed world. As we seek to do ministry in a postmodern context, perhaps the Lord will answer our prayers by enabling us to envision the possibilities of "A Fifth Way."

Appendix C

Reflections on Scripture in a Postmodern Age

The first Christians sought to ground their proclamation of the gospel in ancient Jewish texts as they grappled with the implications of the incarnation. It was necessary, in other words, to make sense of Jesus' life and ministry from within the framework God had already provided.

Eventually, the message of Jesus, which was initially spread by word of mouth, came to take a more permanent form in the various letters of the New Testament. As a result, the writings which told and explicated the story of Jesus were identified and, along with the Old Testament, became the basis for church doctrine and life.

Though the Bible has not always received the serious treatment it deserves, the church has, at its best moments, sought to honor these writings as the special revelation of God's activity and will for His people. It is in this sense that Scripture has always been at the heart of genuine spirituality.

Today, however, postmoderns are challenging believers to rethink the faith, including how best to approach the Bible. Can postmodern thought assist the church in its efforts to rightly relate to Scripture? What follows is a number of suggestions as to how current themes might have a helpful impact on our approach to Scripture.

Scripture in Perspective

Scripture is best interpreted and applied when approached from a community perspective.

While somewhat overgeneralized, we might think of the differences between modernism and postmodernism in these terms: moderns emphasized the individual, whereas postmoderns emphasize community. Our society demonstrates this in many ways, from television shows and movies to everyday life. Scripture reflects this social yearning, calling people into the fellowship of the church. There are parallels, in other words, between the postmodern inclination for community and the Bible's own perspective.

A bibliology that is informed by postmodern tendencies can learn from this community theme. If God has called his people to be one, and if we are all recipients of the same divine love, and if he has given to each of us a measure of faith, it only makes sense to pay heed to what others are saying. This can come in many forms, including dialogue with our neighbors, a receptivity to other theological positions, and a cognizance of the myriad of views that comprise church history.

There are limits, of course, to what any of us can do in our desire to foster an ecumenical spirit. Furthermore, there are dangers along the way, including the temptation to sacrifice the truth in order to avoid offending others. Nevertheless, none of this obviates the general principle of community to which we are called. A right-minded approach to Scripture, therefore, is one in which other relevant parties are invited to the table, a variety of perspectives are allowed into the conversation, and like-minded believers seek to comprehend their sacred texts within an atmosphere of reasonable discussion, healthy debate, and Christ-centered love.

Humility should govern our approach to Scripture.

Contrary to those who make overly confident assertions, postmoderns are skeptical about the human ability to know. Thus, overly detailed (and overly confident?) statements about God are viewed with suspicion. Indeed, the increased pluralism of our day has caused many to wonder whether we can truly know anything with certainty.

Christians can learn something from this ambivalence toward knowledge claims. At the very least–in light of the various denominational distinctions, church feuds, and doctrinal disagreements–the church must face up to the fact that truth is not always easily identified. To the degree that postmoderns have drawn attention to the limitations inherent to all human knowing, it is time to view our Scriptural interpretations with a greater sense of humility. After all, how else should we approach this revelation, given the fact that it contains the wisdom of our Creator and points to mysteries that defy human comprehension?

As we read the Bible, preach sermons, discuss theology, and formulate a perspective on Scripture, it is essential that we do so with an attitude of genuine meekness. Though it would be self-defeating to treat Scripture as if it were undecipherable, and while the big picture is adequately clear, many things warrant continued reflection and an attitude of openness to what the Lord may yet reveal. A postmodern approach to Scripture, therefore, follows the dictum of Scripture itself, which states that the Lord honors those "who tremble at His Word" (Isaiah 66:5).

The stories of Scripture (along with accompanying propositions) must be given greater priority.

Evangelicals have specialized in propositional truth, treating Scripture at times as if its primary use is to be a resource from which various principles or theological statements might be extracted. In a sense, then, there is a tendency among some interpreters to give higher priority to their formulations and doctrinal statements derived from the text than to the text itself. Obviously, postmoderns see things differently, preferring a story to an outline, a personal narrative to an impersonal grouping of facts.

This insight is especially relevant for followers of Jesus who seek to navigate our postmodern world, for Scripture itself is a grand story. The history of the nation of Israel, the ministry of Jesus, and the activity of the early church–all of these contain a wealth of truth in narrative form.

How, then, should we view Scripture? As a series of propositions? In terms of disconnected stories? Neither of these will do, for the only truly valid approach to Scripture is one in which propositions, the truth claims of Scripture (and, in a derivative sense, those drawn *from* Scripture), are held together with the grand biblical story from which they originate. Propositions both flow from and help inform narrative, while narrative contains and gives expression to propositions.

To the degree that postmodernism has accentuated this missing dimension, the church can be thankful. As believers affirm and learn to better appreciate the narrative flavor of God's Word, they will come to connect their own stories to those found in Scripture. In as much as God has chosen to provide stories, our embrace of the biblical narrative is designed to encourage encounters with the master Story-Teller.

The desire to know and apply Scripture is an on-going process.

Modern Christians, captivated by scientific precision and discovery, often failed to recognize that a commitment to God and his Word does not necessitate a static view of what he has revealed. Though the Bible can be sufficiently deciphered, our knowledge of its contents is nowhere near perfect (and won't be this side of heaven). Furthermore, there are many truths, theological truths, that defy our ability to grasp (one thinks of the trinity, the hypostatic union, and the sovereignty of God, to name but a few).

While evangelicals have sometimes treated the Bible as a handbook given to provide support for already well-constructed doctrinal statements, postmoderns with their penchant for process may provide another way of relating to Scripture. Just as life is a journey, so our understanding and application of the Bible are on-going.

What this means for the church is that we need not treat our interpretations as unassailable, especially when it comes to those facets of the faith that have been debated for millennia. Though it would be unwise to put everything "up for grabs," it is equally foolish to act like we have come to a finalized version of doctrine or theology.

A healthier, postmodern-oriented stance entails both confidence that the major truths of God's Word are clear enough and a receptivity to new insights (both from Scripture and regarding how we relate to it). In this sense postmodernism might motivate believers to return to a paradigm in which faith is a pilgrimage and each day is an opportunity to spiral closer to that perfected knowledge that awaits the end of the age.

Scripture and the God of Scripture are best kept together.

Modern theologians and exegetes often separated the biblical from the devotional. While perhaps giving lip-service to the practical matters of life, their actual handling of texts placed a barrier or a hurdle between the Bible and a relationship with its central character.

Of course postmoderns are distrustful of any merely theoretical approach to anything. "Show me" is one of their favorite sayings. While it would be improper to reduce Christianity to a list of moral platitudes, it is nonetheless true that the broad purpose of Scripture is only realized when we give expression to its teachings. This includes access not only to theoretical dogma, facts about the faith, but to an actual encounter with spiritual realities, especially the supreme spiritual reality, the living God.

Our stance toward Scripture, therefore, can only be "on target" to the degree that we encounter that to which Scripture points, namely a (never perfect, yet life-shaping) relationship with our Maker. More so, Scripture itself endorses the notion that our relationship with God's Word requires divine illumination. Thus, for instance, the psalmist implores God to open the eyes of his servant, grant understanding, and revive his thinking (Psalm 119:18-19, 25, 27). In other words clarifying and applying God's Word requires the assistance of its divine Author.

Conclusion

The church's perspective on Scripture is complicated and multi-faceted. Epistemology, biblical authority, the role of tradition, the significance of culture, and the meaning of inspiration are all subjects requiring further exploration. The remarks made here are preliminary efforts to set the tone for those discussions.

In seeking a postmodern way to read Scripture, it would be inappropriate to forget what previous generations have bequeathed the church; God's people have a rich (and varied) theological heritage. The basic point made here is that God is also at work today. Thus, to the degree that postmodern themes are valid, it would be wise to ask how these themes might be brought to bear on the way believers relate to God's Word.

While God does not change, his way of dealing with people often does. Likewise, though God's Word will outlast heaven and earth (Mark 13:31), those of us who live on earth (in anticipation of heaven) must put forth every effort to properly relate to the Bible in our day. What is being advocated here is a view in which believers are open to multiple perspectives, humility is a non-negotiable trait, God's story–and our part in it–is highlighted, new insights are always welcome, and our way of reading Scripture is consistently God-centered.

Bibliography

Anderson, Ray S. *The Shape of Practical Theology: Empowering Ministry with Theological Praxis.* Downers Grove, IL: InterVarsity Press, 2001.

Anderson, Walter Truett. *Reality Isn't What It Used to Be: Theatrical Politics, Ready-to-Wear Religion, Global Myths, Primitive Chic, and Other Wonders of the Postmodern World.* San Francisco, CA: Harper & Row Publishers, 1990.

Bloesch, Donald G. *A Theology of Word & Spirit: Authority & Method in Theology.* Downers Grove, IL: InterVarsity Press, 1992.

Bock, Darrell L. *Purpose Driven Theology: Getting Our Priorities Right in Evangelical Controversies.* Downers Grove, IL: InterVarsity Press, 2002.

Braaten, Carl E., Robert W. Jenson, eds. *The Strange New World of the Gospel: Re-Evangelizing in the Postmodern World.* Grand Rapids, MI: William B. Eerdmans Publishing Company, 2002.

Cairns, Earle E. *Christianity Through The Centuries: A History of the Christian Church.* Grand Rapids, MI: Zondervan Publishing House, 1981.

Carson, D. A. *Divine Sovereignty and Human Responsibility: Biblical Perspective in Tension.* Grand Rapids, MI: Baker Books, 1981.

_____. *The Gagging of God: Christianity Confronts Pluralism.* Grand Rapids, MI: Zondervan Publishing House, 1996.

_____. *The Difficult Doctrine of the Love of God.* Wheaton, IL: Crossway Books, 2000.

_____, ed. *Telling the Truth: Evangelizing Postmoderns.* Grand Rapids, MI: Zondervan Publishing House, 2000.

_____. *Becoming Conversant with the Emerging Church: Understanding a Movement and Its Implications.* Grand Rapids, MI: Zondervan, 2005.

Clark, Kelly James. *Return To Reason: A Critique of Enlightenment Evidentialism and a Defense of Reason and Belief in God.* Grand Rapids, MI: William B. Eerdmans Publishing Company, 1990.

Cowan, Steven B., ed. *Five Views on Apologetics.* Grand Rapids, MI: Zondervan Publishing House, 2000.

Craig, William Lane. "A Classical Apologist's Response" in *Five Views on Apologetics.* Grand Rapids, MI: Zondervan Publishing House, 2000.

Dockery, David, ed. *The Challenge of Postmodernism: An Evangelical Engagement,* Second Edition. Grand Rapids, MI: Baker Book House, 2001.

Eldredge, John. *Waking the Dead: The Glory of a Heart Fully Alive.* Nashville, TN: Thomas Nelson Publishers, 2003.

Elwell, Walter A., ed. *Evangelical Dictionary of Biblical Theology.* Grand Rapids, MI: Baker Books, 1996.

Erickson, Millard J. *Christian Theology.* Grand Rapids, MI: Baker Book House, 1985.

_____. *Postmodernizing the Faith: Evangelical Responses to the Challenge of Postmodernism.* Grand Rapids, MI: Baker Books, 1998.

_____. *Truth or Consequences: The Promise and Perils of Postmodernism.* Downers Grove, IL: InterVarsity Press, 2001.

_____. *The Postmodern World: Discerning the Times and the Spirit of Our Age*. Wheaton, IL: Crossway Books, 2002.

Ferguson, Sinclair B., David F. Wright, eds. *New Dictionary of Theology*. Downers Grove, IL: InterVarsity Press, 1988.

Frame, John M. *The Doctrine of the Knowledge of God: A Theology of Lordship*. Phillipsburg, NJ: Presbyterian and Reformed Publishing Company, 1987.

_____. *The Doctrine of God: A Theology of Lordship*. Phillipsburg, NJ: Presbyterian and Reformed Publishing Company, 2002.

Frost, Michael and Alan Hirsch. *The Shaping of Things to Come: Innovation and Mission for the 21st Century Church*. Peabody, MA: Hendrickson Publishers, 2003.

Fryling, Bob. *Being Faithful in This Generation: The Gospel and Student Culture at the End of the 20th Century*. Downers Grove, IL: InterVarsity Press, 1995.

Greer, Robert C. *Mapping Postmodernism: A Survey of Christian Options*. Downers Grove, IL: InterVarsity Press, 2003.

Grenz, Stanley J. *Revisioning Evangelical Theology: A Fresh Agenda for the 21st Century*. Downers Grove, IL: InterVarsity Pres, 1993.

_____. *Theology for the Community of God*. Nashville, TN: Broadman & Holman Publishers, 1994.

_____. *A Primer on Postmodernism*. Grand Rapids, MI: William B. Eerdmans Publishing Company, 1996.

_____. *Created For Community: Connecting Christian Belief with Christian Living*, Second Edition. Grand Rapids, MI: Baker Books, 1998.

_____. *Renewing the Center: Evangelical Theology in a Post-Theological Era*. Grand Rapids, MI: Baker Book House, 2002.

Grenz, Stanley J. and John R. Franke. *Beyond Foundationalism: Shaping Theology in a Postmodern Context.* Louisville, KY: Westminster John Knox Press, 2002.

Groothuis, Douglas. *Truth Decay: Defending Christianity Against the Challenges of Postmodernism.* Downers Grove, IL: InterVarsity Press, 2000.

Gundry, Stanley N., ed. *Four Views on Salvation in a Pluralistic Word.* Grand Rapids, MI: Zondervan Publishing House, 1995, 1996.

Hayes, Ed. *The Church: The Body of Christ in the World Today.* Nashville, TN: Word Publishers, 1999.

Hegeman, David Bruce. *Plowing in Hope: Toward a Biblical Theology of Culture.* Moscow, ID: Canon Press, 1999.

Hovestol, Tom. *Extreme Righteousness: Seeing Ourselves in the Pharisees.* Chicago, IL: Moody Press, 1997.

Irwin, William, ed. *The Matrix and Philosophy: Welcome to the Desert of the Real.* Chicago and La Salle, IL: Open Court Publishing Company, 2002.

Jones, Tony. *Postmodern Youth Ministry: Exploring Cultural Shift, Cultivating Authentic Community, Creating Holistic Connections.* Grand Rapids, MI: Zondervan, 2001.

Kallenberg, Brad J. *Live to Tell: Evangelism in a Postmodern World.* Grand Rapids, MI: Baker book House, 2002.

Kenneson, Philip D. *Beyond Sectarianism: Re-Imagining Church and World.* Harrisburg, PA: Trinity Press International, 1999.

Kimball, Dan *The Emerging Church: Vintage Christianity for New Generations.* Grand Rapids, MI: Zondervan Publishing House, 2003.

Knight, Henry H. III. *A Future for Truth: Evangelical Theology in a Postmodern World.* Nashville, TN: Abington Press, 1997.

Kruse, Colin G. "The Letters of John" in *The Pillar New Testament Commentary*. Grand Rapids, MI: William B. Eerdmans Publishing Company, 2000.

Long, Jimmy. *Generating Hope: A Strategy for Reaching the Postmodern Generation*. Downers Grove, IL: InterVarsity Press, 1997.

Mayers, Ronald B. *Balanced Apologetics: Using Evidence and Presuppositions in Defense of the Faith*. Grand Rapids, MI: Kregel Publications, 1984.

McLaren, Brian D. *Finding Faith: A Self-Discovery Guide For Your Spiritual Quest*. Grand Rapids, MI: Zondervan Publishing House, 1999.

_____. *The Church on the Other Side: Doing Ministry in the Postmodern Matrix*. Grand Rapids, MI: Zondervan Publishing House, 2000.

_____. *A New Kind of Christian: A Tale of Two Friends on a Spiritual Journey*. San Francisco, CA: Josscy-Bass Books, 2001.

_____. *More Ready Than You Realize: Evangelism as Dance in the Postmodern Matrix*. Grand Rapids, MI: Zondervan, 2002.

_____. *The Story We Find Ourselves In: Further Adventures of a New Kind of Christian*. San Francisco, CA: Jossey-Bass Books, 2003.

_____. *The Last Word and the Word After That: A Tale of Faith, Doubt, and a New Kind of Christianity*. San Francisco, CA: Jossey-Bass Books, 2005.

McLaren, Brian D. and Tony Campolo. *Adventures in Missing the Point: How the Culture-Controlled Church Neutered the Gospel*. Grand Rapids, MI: Zondervan Publishing House, 2003.

McManus, Erwin Raphael. *An Unstoppable Force: Daring to Become the Church God Had in Mind*. Orange, CA: Group Publishing, 2001.

McNeal, Reggie. *The Present Future: Six Tough Questions for the Church*. San Francisco, CA: Jossey-Bass Books, 2003.

McGrath, Alister. *Evangelicalism and the Future of Christianity*. Downers Grove, IL: InterVarsity Press, 1995.

Middleton, J. Richard and Brian J. Walsh. *Truth Is Stranger Than It Used To Be: Biblical Faith in a Postmodern World*. Downers Grove, IL: InterVarsity Press, 1995.

Miller, Donald. *Blue Like Jazz: Nonreligious Thoughts on Christian Spirituality*. Nashville, TN: Thomas Nelson Publishers, 2003.

Miller, Mark. *Experiential Storytelling: (Re)Discovering Narrative to Communicate God's Message*. Grand Rapids, MI: Zondervan Press, 2003.

Moo, Douglas J. "2 Peter and Jude" in *The NIV Application Commentary*. Grand Rapids, MI: Zondervan Publishing Company, 1996.

Morgenthaler, Sally. *Worship Evangelism: Inviting Unbelievers into the Presence of God*. Grand Rapids, MI: Zondervan Publishing House, 1999.

Myers, Joseph R. *The Search to Belong: Rethinking Intimacy, Community, and Small Groups*. Grand Rapids, MI: Zondervan, 2003.

Newbigin, Lesslie. *Foolishness to the Greeks: The Gospel and Western Culture*. Grand Rapids, MI: William B. Eerdmans Publishing Company, 1986.

_____. *Proper Confidence: Faith, Doubt, and Certainty in Christian Discipleship*. Grand Rapids, MI: William B. Eerdmans Publishing Company, 1995.

Osborne, Grant R. *The Hermeneutical Spiral: A Comprehensive Introduction to Biblical Interpretation*. Downers Grove, IL: InterVarsity Press, 1991.

Peace, Richard V. *Conversion in the New Testament: Paul and the Twelve*. Grand Rapids, MI: William B. Eerdmans Publishing Company, 1999.

Peck, M. Scott. *The Different Drum: Community Making and Peace*. New York, NY: Simon & Schuster Publishers, 1987.

Peters, Ted. *God–The World's Future: Systematic Theology for a Postmodern Era*. Minneapolis, MN: Fortress Press, 1992.

Phillips, Timothy R., Dennis L. Okholm, eds. *Christian Apologetics in the Postmodern World*. Downers Grove, IL: InterVarsity Press, 1995.

Poe, Harry Lee. *Christian Witness in a Postmodern World*. Nashville, TN: Abington Press, 2001.

Scalise, Charles J. *From Scripture to Theology: A Canonical Journey into Hermeneutics*. Downers Grove, IL: InterVarsity Press, 1996.

Schaeffer, Francis A. *He Is There and He Is Not Silent: Does It Make Sense to Believe in God?* Wheaton, IL: Tyndale House Publishers, 1980.

Seay, Chris. "I Have Inherited the Faith of My Fathers" in *Stories of Emergence: Moving From Absolute To Authentic*. Grand Rapids, MI: Zondervan Publishing House, 2003.

Seay, Chris and Greg Garrett. *The Gospel Reloaded: Exploring Spirituality and Faith in the Matrix*. Colorado Springs, CO: Pinon Press, 2003.

Smith, Chuck Jr. *The End of the World . . . As We Know It: Clear Directions for Bold and Innovative Ministry in a Postmodern World*. Colorado Springs, CO: WaterBrook Press, 2001.

Sweet, Leonard. *Soul Tsunami: Sink or Swim in New Millennium Culture*. Grand Rapids, MI: Zondervan Publishing House, 1999.

_____. *Postmodern Pilgrims: First Century Passion For the 21ˢᵗ Century World*. Nashville, TN: Broadman & Holman Publishers, 2000.

_____, ed. *The Church in Emerging Culture: Five Perspectives*. Grand Rapids, MI: Zondervan Publishing House, 2003.

Sweet, Leonard, Brian D. McLaren, and Jerry Haselmayer. *A is for Abductive: The Language of the Emerging Church*. Grand Rapids, MI: Zondervan Publishing House, 2003.

Sweeting, George. *Who Said That?* Chicago, IL: Moody Press, 1995.

Tomlinson, Dave. *The Post Evangelical* (Revised North American Edition). Grand Rapids, MI: Zondervan, 2003.

Van Huyssteen, J. Wetzel. *Essays in Postfoundationalist Theology.* Grand Rapids, MI: William B. Eerdmans Publishing Company, 1997.

Webber, Robert E. *Journey To Jesus: The Worship, Evangelism, and Nurture Mission of the Church. Nashville, TN: Abingdon Press, 2001.*

_____. *The Younger Evangelicals: Facing the Challenges of the New World.* Grand Rapids, MI: Baker Books, 2002.

_____. *Ancient-Future Evangelism: Making Your Church a Faith-Forming Community.* Grand Rapids, MI: Baker books, 2003.

Wells, David F. *God in the Wasteland: The Reality of Truth in a World of Fading Dreams.* Grand Rapids, MI: William B. Eerdmans Publishing Company, 1994.

Wood, Ralph C. *Contending for the Faith: The Church's Engagement with Culture.* Waco, TX: Baylor University Press, 2003.

Wood, W. Jay. *Epistemology: Becoming Intellectually Virtuous.* Downers Grove, IL: InterVarsity Press, 1998.

Credits

Leonard Sweet, Postmodern Pilgrims: First Century Passion For the 21st Century World (Nashville, TN: Broadman & Holman Publishers, 2000). Used by permission.

Reprinted by permission of Thomas Nelson Inc., Nashville, TN. From the book BLUE LIKE JAZZ copyright date 2003 by Donald Miller. All rights reserved.

Reprinted from The End of the World as We Know It. Copyright © 2001 by Chuck Smith, jr. Used by permission of WaterBrook Press, Colorado Springs, CO. All rights reserved.

Richard V. Peace, Conversion in the New Testament: Paul and the Twelve (Grand Rapids, MI: William B. Eerdmans Publishing Company, 1999). Used by permission.

Taken from Gagging of God, The by DONALD A. CARSON. Copyright © 1996 by D. A. Carson. Used by permission of The Zondervan Corporation.

Taken from Adventures in Missing the Point by ANTHONY CAMPOLO; BRIAN D. MCLAREN. Copyright © 2003 by Youth Specialties. Used by permission of The Zondervan Corporation.

Taken from Church on the Other Side, The by BRIAN D. MCLAREN. Copyright © 1998, 2000 by Brian D. McLaren. Used by permission of The Zondervan Corporation.

Taken from A is for Abductive by BRIAN D. MCLAREN; LEONARD SWEET; JERRY HASELMEYER. Copyright © 2003 by Leonard I. Sweet, Brian D. McLaren, and Jerry Haselmeyer. Used by permission of The Zondervan Corporation.

If you would like to contact the author, he can be reached at
carmen1978@comcast.net.